William Czappa

How to talk to a Born-Again Republican, Don't!

Talking points for people who are **willing and able** to **comprehend** actual facts on common topics like Immigration, gun control, Single Payer and abortion.

First Edition
September 22, 2019

Published in the United States by;

ARC Publishing.
2529 W. Magnolia
Burbank, Ca. 91505
(818) 846-5820 email
czappasstudio@gmail.com
Web: www.czappasart.com
or Google: czappa

Photo credit and all artwork;
William Czappa

Image credits
Senator Bernie Sanders Campaign
Democrat under ground

ISBN- 9781691057719

Names have been changed to protect the
innocent if any are similar it is purely by accident.
Spelling errors may be intentional or just errors.

Book code 93020191030

Dedication

I would like to dedicate this book to all the people who helped me write it by being themselves which challenged me to figure out how they were thinking. And to all the other writers and radio and TV commentators that filled in the blank spots on all these various topics.

About the Author

William Czappa is a California artist and writer who has made sculptures from found objects since the sixties. He began writing short stories in 1989 and began sending them out to people on his art mailing list. Shortly thereafter he began sending them out to the extensive mailing list for his electronic business in Burbank which he used to support and supplement his art and writing enterprises. That business became a gallery for his artwork, and in fact, it was the oldest art gallery in Burbank as of this writing was open for 35 years.

In 1987 the Burbank Leader Newspaper began printing his short stories along with the Tolucan and to date they have printed over twenty of them. They have also been published on various internet sites devoted to writing. Some articles in his newsletter have also been published in the Burbank Times and the Burbank Leader, Business world and the Latest Magazine. In 1999 the compilation of his short stories was completed and the first run has since been sold out as well as the second edition. He also began writing about consumer products and what was happening to the repair industry and things our government was undermining small business's.

Since then William wrote his second book about his art, including an autobiography and explanations of his art works with over 50 color photos. Since then there have been three documentary shorts made on William and his work, the most recent can be seen on Vimeo.

That video has been shown in three film festivals and became a Vimeo staff pick and was viewed over 34,000 times and posted on other sites, filling 10 Google pages and having been seen across the world. It was also picked up by National Geographic's on line videos of people doing things in the world

To date he has written 7 books, including a book on what he had learned repairing things in the repair industry, "Tech Techniques." He sold his business in 2017 and realized he had learned a lot about running a small business so he wrote about how to run a successful small business. And for over 18 years he had sold things on eBay for himself and others, so he also wrote the "eBay users handbook" which is selling sell on Amazon.

And since Facebook became popular, he began a journey of debating subjects as they came up on that site. After many years of filling in the blanks, paying attention and listening to others, he realized he had something to offer the public. People that didn't have the time to dive deeply into the various issues of the day. He had been making the same arguments on these various topics for years and realized, why not just cut and paste. He had already written the book via his comments to people on Facebook! And so there it all was, this book documenting reasonable talking points of the issues of our day.

And, in this journey, he realized that there was indeed something very wrong with certain types of people. For overall ten years he tried to figure it out and finally made a break through. There is something very different about certain types of people in the realm of politics. The Born-Again-Republican is a anomaly and all explained in this book.

Preface

After listening and posting things on face book and having email discussions now for well over 15 years, I realized that there were people out there, some close friends, that I could no longer have a normal conversation with. Some had disconnected with me in fact. So this was puzzling, what had changed? Some of these same people went to Ross Pero events with me our signed petitions for the legalization for marijuana in the 70's. But now they had become "Republicans" and we could no longer converse on the same subjects. And what was even more disconcerning was they were supporting ideas that where very different than the ideas we had shared when we were younger. Some had gone to Vietnam protesting events but were now supporting the same kind of people that made Viet Nam possible! What was going on here?

I new that Newt Gingridege decided to not do any more "compromising" with the democrats. He was going on the attack and they could not agree on things any more. In fact Mitch McConnell, on 60 minutes years later, could not even utter the word, **compromise**, he could only say, **common ground**. They could only agree on things that would benefit both parties.

So then enters Rush and Fox and Prager, the spin doctors, who would whip this new base up into a frenzy. The liberal democrats and Mexicans and lazy blacks would become the new enemy. And if you were not one of them, then you must be one of those ignorant Liberal Democrats that need to be wiped off the face of the earth, so said, Rush and Beck. There would be 257 news talk stations owned by the top five companies. 2,570 Hours of **conservative talk** broadcast by those radio stations every day.

Like MTV, that was a failure in the beginning, but went back and found out what kids really wanted and then became very successful with what they had found. What did they find out? kids wanted, sex, drugs and rock and roll. And they gave it to them. Nothing about, getting a good job, making money, belong to a successful group or business. Nothing about the kid who did well in school and was now starting a major corporation with an innovative product he built in his garage.

And that's what these Republican shows did too. They put out what their <u>base</u> wanted to hear. Often the people in Fox's base were successful, because they were the ones not listening to M TV and they got good jobs and "made it," in their view anyway. And they didn't want to share anything with all those lazy people who just want hand outs, that want to buy lobster and booze with their welfare checks. And all those Mexicans breaking the law and stealing our good paying jobs, you now those really good jobs picking lettuce, making beds, mowing lawns, washing cars, those good paying jobs!

Now, here we are, a country divided on purpose I think, but one side can't see it. They have become like zombies repeating what they heard on their "shows." *Fox is the only news show you have to listen too,"* so they said.

I wasn't the only ones noticing this, Bill Mayer had a segment on his show where he tried to talk to a man in a bubble. Anyone living in a bubble can't hear what you're saying.

Now to dive into this may lay, I had to dig deep and for years I was trying to figure this out in different ways. I first thought that civil conversation had just died. Then I realized that one party was acting differently than the other and thought maybe they had become a cult, because they seemed to be acting that way.

VII

Then talking with a friend, he pointed out the one thing that really hit home, **implants.** And there it was, it did have a connection with religion in some way, but the Born-Again religious person was not the cause, but under the same spell of the implant which was like a hypnotic suggestion that they could not disobey.

And so that is my theory and I'm sticking to it, till I find some evidence that it isn't true. Everything seems to fit that scenario. So let's see if it makes sense to you too.

My philosophy is this on any subject. I have a working hypotheses, based on the data that I currently have, but I'm always open to new relevant data.

VIII

Status Quo

Index

Section 1

Section 2

Common Discussions Regarding Healthcare

Section 3

Various Topical Current Talking Points

<u>Section 4</u>

What kind of Government have we Become

<u>**Section 1**</u>

Chapter 1

Introducing the Born-Again Republican

For some time now I've been trying to figure out why it's so difficult to talk to what I'll now call, **The Born-Again Republican** (Not all Republicans come under this heading, just the ones that exhibit the tendencies I am about to explain). I'll use that phrase because there is a similarity there to religion. If you have ever tried to talk to a Born-Again Christian, Jehovah Witness or a Moonie, you know what I'm talking about. No matter what you try to say or explain on how you feel and why you won't be joining their church, you will still be told that, "If you don't accept Jesus right now, you will be going to hell." Even making a joke by saying, "I'm already in hell, I live in Los Angeles," won't even get through to them, they won't even laugh.

So it's the same with the Born-Again Republican. No matter what facts or <u>reasonable </u>points of view you come up with to prove a point, will be unacknowledged and deflected (This also answers the question as to why "Facts" are now in contention). If cornered they will change the subject or go on the attack. I actually compiled a list of these techniques that they use. The rest of them are in appendix 4 under, **How to find if your living in a cult**.

Here are a few of them.

If you disagree with them, they'll call you a democrat or liberal with a tone level, as if everyone knows, that's a bad thing.

*They never consider that you could be **independent** or a member of the Green party or some other party.*

If you make a good point they won't acknowledge it but will change the subject instead or invalidate the source of your data.

They will blame the other party for everything that's wrong with the country and believe that their guy is the only one who can fix everything. And they'll believe that, even though he has had many many failure's.

They can never admit that their guy ever did anything wrong or the opposite guy ever did anything right.

They accuse the opposite party with gross generalities, they <u>always</u> raise taxes, they <u>always</u> start wars, they always <u>lie</u> etc.

And get this, they did not all go to the same school and learn these deflection techniques, but most of them use the same techniques? How did that happen? It's as if they're running on automatic. And what's interesting is this, most of them will all be in agreement on these same topics, immigration, welfare, the wall, against Single Payer and abortion, voter ID, against Socialism etc. Other people may be against Single Payer but might be for Right to Choose. But no, they will usually be in lock step on all these same issues.

Now this brings me to the basic thing that's wrong with them that I discovered. There is a thing called an **implant**. Many people have ideas that have been implanted in their subconscious minds. I'm not going into where they came from here, that's a whole other story. I can say this though, it was discovered by people practicing regression therapy.

But I can give you an idea of what I'm talking about though. One good way to understand it is hypnotism. A person who has been hypnotized, then told by the hypnotist to cough every time the hypnotist touches his nose, then is told to wake up but not remember what was said in the session. And the person cannot stop coughing every time the hypnotist touches his nose. He has no idea that there is a connection.

Another explanation of this phenomena is a person who keeps washing their hands, or has to drive the same way to work every day, they can't help themselves, something in their mind is making them do these things. You may have met someone who seems to be totally normal, successful and interesting, but then on one or two particular subjects they go off the rails and become irrational on those subjects. You try to talk to them about it to understand why they are that way on **that subject**, but you get know where. In fact, **most therapies are trying to find hidden things in the subconscious mind.**

And that's what an implant really is, but it was put there some time in the past and the person doesn't know it's there. Something in present time can re-stimulate it and it turns on and that person has no control over it or his actions. There are all kinds of implants, like religious implants for instance, that can be re-stimulated simply by seeing colors shinning through a stained glass window. That may be why stained glass windows in churches are so popular, the pastors are unknowingly re-stimulating a religious implant.

They can be re-stimulated by a rousing talk in an event at a stadium. Certain types of cadence in a speech can trigger them. When they studied Hitler's speeches, they discovered a hypnotic like pattern to them. It was also discovered that Vaughner's Symphonies used this same cadence as he used. It would start slow, then build, then go slow again, then build. It could be Trumps many events fulfill that purpose too.

And when you see someone with one of them in re-stimulation, you can almost see a glassy look in their eyes. It takes over their mind and it's as if you're talking to some sort of circuit. Their reasoning mind has turned off and all that's running is the ideas or data that is contained in the implant. It's as if a tape is playing. You know LRH had a great definition of sanity and that is this, "The ability to recognize Differences, Similarities and Identities." And people who can't do that are to that degree, insane. The implant turns all or some of those abilities off.

So for instance, they are often found blaming poor people for taking food stamps or being on welfare. "They shouldn't be cheating us!" they'll say. So you point out the much bigger **similar** problem of corporations taking handouts. Fossil fuel subsidies range from $10 Million to $52 Million annually. The ratio is 36 for food stamps to 870 for government subsidies. But to them, only the lower number will be what they're concerned with.

Now if they were really concerned about government handouts, **similar** information should register. But it doesn't! They often won't even comment on it, they'll ignore it. A normal person would at least say, yeah that's a problem too! And they might start mentioning it to others as well on Facebook or in emails to friends. But the Born-Again will seldom, if ever do that.

Part of the reason it doesn't resister is this, they are listening to the same news sources that are drilling these ideas in, they're **re-stimulating** them. And those news sources are God to them. So if their God is not talking about it, the subject doesn't actually exist for them. They're only going to listen and regurgitate what their preacher told them. And if you're not with them, then you're the enemy, you're the devil and can't be trusted.

So the reason there seems to be more of them around today is the proliferation of these spin doctor news sources that are constantly re-stimulating them.

I tried to make a point to a Born-Again relative that 20 soldiers a day were committing suicide. Because he already target me as "The Enemy" he couldn't believe this information, it didn't come over his channels so it couldn't be true. I found an article on the net that showed it was true and sent it to him. He said he didn't believe it because it came from a Liberal site. I went back and found the most Conservative sit I could find that mentioned it and he couldn't accept that either because, I found the site. A month later, it apparent showed up on one of his "trusted" sources and he finally agreed it was true. That's how much effort it took to make him agree to one single point

The spin doctors (Just like many religions say, "**They are the only way)"**make sure their flock does not read, tune in or listen to anyone who is in opposition to the Republican platform. They know who the people are who are spilling the beans on their rhetoric. So they have to cut them off at the pass. They can't have them reading or listening to them because it would blow the whole show. So they have to invalidate them and make them the enemy. They have to make them the "fake news." Most of their members not only wouldn't think of listening to a Michael Moore movie or read any of the numerous books, TV and radio shows critical of their party or its policies, but they sure want you to listen to theirs. And boy if you want to stay informed, you should tune in occasionally so you really know what they're saying and doing. It's important to know how they operate.

But the Born-Again doesn't have that ability. They would never consider listening to any of them to find out for themselves, because they trust their source fully. I offered to play a Moore movie once to one of them and it was like I was trying to poison him.

But I just had to watch the movie, "Michael Moore Hates America." Filmed by a Born-Again for the purpose of invalidating him, because he is one of many big sources of exposing what's really going on.

This guys movie was mostly silly, but he did make a few good points, mostly about how Michael exaggerates things in his movies. For instance, in one scene in "Bowling for Columbine" Michael was talking about a bank that was giving away a rifle if you opened a bank account with them. But you had to pick the gun up somewhere else. But he filmed it as if he got the gun from the bank and walked out the front door with it. It would have been nice if Michael had told us that. But the important facts in the story where actually true, a bank was giving away rifles.

While on the subject, that's another thing you find with them, if you don't agree with them, you just **hate America** and should just leave instead of working to make it better.

So there's really no way to get through to them short of running out the implant. The implant makes them listen to the same kinds of news shows too. And I think these shows, particularly Fox shows, Hannity and Rush are almost like being in church listening to a sermon. Before Hannity there was Glenn Beck who became so nuts, even Fox had to let him go. You just can't go on TV, even Fox TV, and say things like, "They should kill all the liberals." Rush Limbaugh once **quipped**," I tell people: "Don't kill all the liberals. Leave enough so we can have two on every campus—living fossils—so we will never forget what these people stood for." Somehow he's still on the air.

But Fox is not <u>news</u>, it's just a continuous put down and haranguing of the other party. But they have not realized that yet. Mean while, Fox ignores anything bad Trump or Republicans have done. They are at best a news spinning services. When they started they had a news room like set, but no real reporters that went out in the field investigating stories, they just read from the news feeds and spun it pretending to be a real news service.

One day I happened to be watching one of the panel shows on Fox when Obama was president. They were talking about his good employment numbers when one of the guys on the couch pulls out a letter from the RNC. And he reads it on the air. It said, "Don't talk about Obama's good employment numbers talk about his failures." He then said, "Yeah what about etc" and went into some conflict Obama was dealing with.

So you really cannot have a conversation with the Born-Again-Republican on political subjects. You can discuss all kinds of other things though without having a problem. You should not re-stimulate them. You can be antagonistic but all that'll do is turn on the implant even more and they'll eventually disconnect from you. Seven of them have done that to me so far and two of them I new from grade school.

It's also possible that you might find a democrat like this too. I've been told they exist, usually by a Born-Again-Republican, but so far, I have not found one but they probably exist, I've been looking. I pretended to be a Republican and posted things on posts that were clearly pro liberal to see if I could find one. I did find one that was critical of Trump and said something like, "What a great guy, he is work so hard for all of us." But all I got was comments like this, "Your joking right?" They all thought I was just making a joke and not being serious. And these were not people who new me. And it just may be that there are far less Liberal radio and TV shows out there re-stimulating them.

There really is nothing you're going to say that will turn them around, so don't even try. And that's very hard to do, because many subjects can pull you in. If you say your business is not doing well, they'll say, "Oh, now that Trump's in the economy is going to be doing just fine." And there you go, easy to be pulled in.

But you can and should do this.
"This is the real purpose of this book."

Say you're having a Facebook discussion on some topic, you may be able to make points with everyone else that might be listening in though. And that's no small thing, because there're so many people out there that don't dig in and study issues deeply. So **those people can be swayed either way** and it's important to do that, now more than ever. Just remember to do it gently and not get antagonistic and turn it into a fight as that will just turn off everyone specially the people you're trying to reach. You could say, things like this, "But have you considered this point?" "But, isn't it true that so and so," "Could it be that etc" Get the idea? Just gently fill in the missing data.

The rest of this book will be devoted to arguments or talking points or discussions you can make for common topics and hopefully wake up the other people that are not Born-Agains.

In fact, if you have this book on Kendal you can just cut and paste these various talking points and save yourself a lot of time. But don't think for a minute you'll make points with a Born-Again. **And don't let it get you down, now that you know what you're dealing with, just let it go.** And just enjoy the "likes" you'll get from the others. I was told just this evening as I'm writing this that a young family friend really enjoys my comments and posts, but he never even sent me a like. So you don't know who's listening to your posts. Write them as if the whole world is listening in.

So the trick is to keep the conversation going with the Born-Again as long as you can. Keep calmly making your points even though they are not listening. Just keep filling in the blanks. You may find more of them chiming in with the usual comments and calling you a demented Liberal, but just keep filling in the blanks. I never take overt abuse though, I just block those types.

And sometimes you might be wrong on a subject too. Even the Born-Again can make a good point on some topic you might not have thought about, acknowledge it, learn from it, admit the error and move on.

Section 2

Common Discussions Involving Healthcare

The American Healthcare System

9

Chapter 2

Is Single Payer Really Socialism?

The reality is Socialism, so what? Isn't buying insurance from a corporation like Socialism, money is being pooled together? What's the difference? The only difference is either a corporation is managing it (And making a huge profit off it, like over 200 billion a year) or our government is managing it. Neither one is perfect, they both make mistakes. But the very important point is this, Single Payer <u>will be cheaper</u> if managed properly and here's why.

Even the Koch brothers recent study, and several others, showed that Single Payer would be cheaper than what we have now. And that's not hard to see. First of all, because of Reagan's hospital mandate that said, "**No one could be turned away from an emergency room**," which means we are already a **Single payer System!** That effectively is Socialism and a **Single Payer** and everyone is covered already, including illegal immigrants. Who's paying for it? All of us through higher taxes and higher hospital and insurance costs. That's why a band aid costs $10.00 in a hospital. The problem is this, that's the most expensive way to provide healthcare because if you handle a medical problem **before it gets worse**, that saves money, sometimes lots of money. **Emergency room care is the most expensive way to provide care.**

The other reason it's cheaper is this, insurance companies rake in 30% right off the top, so there is a 30% savings right there. Not to mention how much time doctors and nurses

nurses have to spend filling out forms and arguing with the insurance companies to get things approved.

That's a huge cost to hospitals and private medical offices. And if you could also handle the outrageous prices drug companies charge, you can see that Single Payer would be a huge savings.

Sometimes pooling our money together just makes sense and we can save money by having a Single Payer system. If you want to call that "Socialism" then so be it, but realize **what we have now is already Single Payer, it's already Socialism, just a very expensive inefficient Socialism**.

Why not move to a more **efficient** and **cheaper** system? That's why our healthcare system is always rated 30th in the world of developed countries. We spend the most money with the worst result and the least amount of people covered.

And sadly, it has been suggested, many times, that some Born-Again Republicans don't want it is because brown and black people will be covered. And of course **they're already covered**, but you can't tell them that, they can't see how it is **similar.**

Chapter 3

You Won't be Able to Keep Your Doctor Discussion

We already lost that ability. With most insurance policies you have to go to their doctor or their hospital. I needed to go to a Urgent Care for something, I had to first call my insurance company to make sure I was covered there. Then once there, the doctor wanted a specialist on staff to look at my problem, but he had to make sure the other doctor was on my plan. He wasn't, so he couldn't be consulted, so they had to send me to the emergency room instead. Urgent Care of course billed my insurance company anyway. In fact, I got home after visiting them and noticed another related problem, so I returned. Urgent care billed my insurance company a second time, they changed the date though on the second visit so they could get away with it.

Then Urgent Care tried to bill me too, saying my insurance didn't cover them after all. I finally had to get them both on the phone together to figure it all out. Hours of wasted time. Turns out there are sub insurance companies involved in my Heath net Advantage Medicare plan. They finally covered it. But really, three different insurances companies involved? How efficient is that?

Chapter 4

They will have Death Squads if we have Single Payer

We already have death squads because the insurance company makes money by denying care. I was listening to a hearing on TV in Washington awhile back. Doctors were testifying that, they were paid a bonus if they denied care. One doctor thought, it went against his Hippocratic Oath and so quite that job, after denying care for years and collecting all those commissions, and now he was spilling the beans. I guess to compensate for all the people he harmed or killed. 26,000 people die each year from lack of health insurance and the free emergency room couldn't help them.

Here are some more numbers on this subject per Google.

In 2013, the average **uninsured** person had half the amount of medical expenditures as the average insured person ($2,443 versus $4,876). In 2013, the **cost** of "uncompensated care" provided to **uninsured** individuals was $84.9 billion. Uncompensated care includes health care services without a direct source of payment. May 30, 2014

Troublesome News: Numbers Of **Uninsured** On The Rise. As of **May 2018**, the numbers of people in the **U.S. without health insurance** have risen to 15.5%, up from 12.7% two years ago, according to the latest Commonwealth Fund tracking survey. This translates to an increase of four million **uninsured** people nationwide. Jul 6, 2018

Chapter 5

The Government Can't Do Anything Right, Right?

This one is funny because the government does a lot of things right, like World War 1 and World War 2. They're often the same people anyway running these agencies. So why is it you get hired by the government and you suddenly become incompetent? But it also assumes the private sector does things better and that's not true either. The number of people dying because of blunders at private hospitals is 250,000 each year. And doctors and nurses, are our most trained professionals!

But look at the numbers or pieces of mail that get delivered each day by the post office. I have done a lot of eBay sales for over the last 18 years and thus have done a lot of shipping and I've found the US post office to be the best overall. They even have the best price for packages up to 2 lbs. Here are some amazing stats on what they do per Google.

The Postal Service adds 4,071 addresses to their delivery network every day. Each day the Postal Service processes and delivers 187. 8 million pieces of First-Class Mail. On average, the Postal Service processes 20.2 million mail pieces each hour, 336,649 each minute and 5,611 each second. Still think our government can't do anything right?

And by the way, UPS routes some of its packages through USPS for shipping. Apparently it's cheaper for them to use USPS for some routes.

Note; these same people saying the government can't run anything right will never ever confront the pentagon though. They're just fine with what's going on there. The military can't do anything wrong! They'll never ever suggest we do an audit on them.

Side note: The one thing that's wrong with the postal service is this. People in high places insisted that they fund their retirement fund till 2036. Which makes it look like they're in financial trouble. Why did they do that? Because the people that past that bill want to privatize it. Why? So they can get their greedy little hands on all that money they make. More on that later.

Chapter 6

You Will have Long Lines Waiting for Healthcare, People Will Die

There are already lines. If you have private insurance you have to wait for your company to approve the procedure. Often, they may have you try cheaper alternatives first so they can save money. And many people have their procedure denied and end up dead, there is no longer waiting line then being dead! And, for people who can't afford insurance or pay for their care, you're going to wait in line. People in countries with single payer are finding they're living 5 years longer than us and spending over all ½ as much. Our life expectancy has not risen much since the 70's.

But it's estimated that at least 45,000 people die annually because they don't have and can't afford healthcare insurance. Even Obama care left some 20 million out in the cold and not covered.

And healthcare should include **living cleaner**. I had an employee that was drinking, smoking and eating badly, yet waiting in line to have his second angioplasty for heart disease. If you're going to abuse your body, then you should be denied care. In the beginning there was talk about this in Obama Care, but that never got included. Apparently the fast food industry, a major player in our bad health numbers, had a say in it. Just a wild guess.

Chapter 7

Who's Pushing the Idea that This Would be Bad Because it's Socialism?

Who is pumping out "Run, Socialism is coming?" The insurance companies of course. They're cleaning our clocks and doing everything to hold down their costs by denying care while increasing co pays and insurance rates. The biggest cost in most people's lives is their healthcare costs. And those companies see where we are headed, **Single Payer**, and they are investing in other companies to protect their interests. Unfortunately for us, some of those companies are drug companies.

No, it's really the Capitalist System which we should be suspicious of. If a capitalist system really worked, we wouldn't be having this discussion. We would all be covered at an affordable rate and our system wouldn't be ranked 30th in the world. We'd be living longer. And, we really don't have Capitalism any more anyway. We have instead become "Crony Capitalists." More on how Capitalism has failed us and is feeding on our bones later.

Section 3

Various Topical Current Talking Points

Antipasta

Chapter 8

A Discussion on Abortion

This is an area where the Born-Again Republican goes the craziest and become the most irrational. On the one hand, they want to reveres Row Versus Wade, which was the key legislation that made abortions legal in 1973. But you'll not get anywhere with them with any logical arguments about this subject. And there are some good arguments that can be made starting with this, when it was illegal there were still abortions being done, many in back rooms, many botched with woman dying and deformed babies being born that didn't get aborted.

Another is, it really only applies to poorer people that can't afford to raise a kid. Wealthier people can afford to simply leave the state or the country for their abortion, (And they will) so it really is only a penalty for being poor. Some of them even want to really intrude in people's lives by making it illegal to leave the state or country for an abortion. How would they do that? Make doctors report on them? Now remember, these are the same people that are all for "smaller" government and "State's Rights" and against government "intrusion" into our lives. But they have no problem banning abortions but banning assault rifles that are massacring our living children is not ok.

And of course, Republicans don't want to pay for welfare either, but want poor people to have more kids? What? But they also don't want to pay for, sex education or contraception, or even paid maternal leave either? Things that have been shown to keep abortions from happening in other countries.

Some church groups will help out for the first year or so, then, you're on your own. It's estimated that it costs over $200,000. 00 to raise a child and that does not include college. Can you imagine a poor woman alone, or even a poor couple trying to live on a fast food income, not able to leave work for even a day or two, then trying to raise a child with no money, no way to pay for someone to take care of the baby while they have to go to work to make rent (And they want to defund planned parenthood that provides free prenatal care to poor people too).

They don't care about this at all! Their cry is, "**be responsible**." Who's teaching responsibility today? Our schools sure aren't, but they do that in Sweden and the Netherlands and they have a very low teen pregnancy rates. I was born to parents that didn't want another child but the condom broke. And there I was. You can be as "responsible" as you want but contraceptives are not 100%. Luckily for me, they could afford to raise another child, although I occasionally had a feeling that I was unwelcomed.

It's also well know that the more educated a child is, the less likely they will have premarital sex or join a gang. But what do they also work towards? Defunding schools and are against a free or even cheap college education.

Here are some technical facts. In 2015 in the United States, about 1. 3% of abortions took place after the 21st week, and less than 1% occurred after 24 weeks. The reasons for late terminations of pregnancy include, when a pregnant woman's health is at risk or when lethal fetal abnormalities have been detected in the baby.

This just makes me want to pull my hair out (If I wasn't already bald), they don't want abortions yet they don't want to prevent them either? Their conflicting beliefs are causing, **more abortions!**

Chapter 9

The Advantages of Planned Parenthood.
Should it be Defunded?

They want to defund this organization that is actually doing a lot of good for poorer woman who need medical care. By having pre-natal care, you may in fact save some babies that might end up aborting naturally because of some medical issue. They actually prevent 579,000 unintended pregnancies each year. They also save unwanted pregnancy by providing 1.5 million young people with sex education. They also prevent and treat 4. 2 million for sexually transmitted diseases which is 42% of what they do. **Only 3% of what they do is abortions**. They also prevent abortions by providing 2 million contraception kits and do 3,445 vasectomies and 718 female sterilizations procedures each year.

What do Born-Again Republicans want to do? Of course, **get rid of the organization that is preventing the most abortions in the country because of the 3% of abortions that they do!** If anyone can explain the logic of their thinking, please explain it to me because this does not make any sense.

And notice what kind of people who are the most adamant about this, older fat white men. You have to wonder if their real hidden motive is this, they can't get their peckers up anymore, so no one else should have any fun either.

Chapter 10

Opinions on Being Responsible

Now this is also an interesting one. They have a big button on "being responsible." You should be responsible and not abort a baby, you should be "responsible" and not be on welfare. **But that's as far as it goes.** Often they are people who did very well in college and got a great well paid profession or happened to marry the right person, our have an ability that made them easy money, or their parents dropped lots of money in their lap, or they just got lucky with a business and did very well. But because it was so easy for them, they think, "Well I did it, can't everyone do what I did?" No, no, not everyone can do what you did. And it's not that all successful people think like this, just the ones with the implant. Discussing this will not change their mind, not everyone can make it. And our government made it even harder to "make it" by shipping good paying manufacturing jobs out of the country. Those good paying factory jobs helped a lot of people, who would never have been college material, "make it."

But what they never see and don't care about is this, if the politicians they vote for, and are supporting, are being "responsible." Is it responsible to give a huge tax breaks to people that are already filthy rich and then make up for it by taking things away from the poor and handicapped people? Is it being responsible to deny climate change?

And not only deny it, but make things worse by supporting things that make it worse and defunding things that make it better, like solar? Or invade a country that never bothered us like Iraqi? Where is your "reasonability" by voting for irresponsible people?

They don't care, they only care that the poor person doesn't abort that baby she can't afford to raise. And will they step up to the plate to help out, maybe sometimes, for the first year maybe. There are 40,000 children in foster care in the USA. How about a little help?

Chapter 11

Charities Should Handle the Poor, Not the Government

First of all, way back to Bush senior, remember him saying this? "A thousand points of light" which meant, all the churches and charities should help the needy, not the government. And even back then, those organizations were overwhelmed. If they could have handled it, we wouldn't have 45 million people living without enough food in our country. We wouldn't have an ever increasing number of people living on our streets. This was just an excuse so the government could get out of its "responsibility" to take care of its people who fell between the cracks, often because of their **very own polices**.

Why should they take care of their people? Because they created the problem in the first place when they shipped all those good paying manufacturing jobs to Mexico and China. Now they want to take milk out of the mouths of poor babies, cut meals on wheels etc. Mean while, they can't find enough ways to shower rich people with more government funded money? Why is it that the same people who are so worried about poor people accepting welfare never ever mention rich people and corporations taking billions of government money? Why is that? **Implants** and the inability to notice things that are **similar** .

Image from Democrat under ground

And often these same people think that it's mostly black people, and other minorities, using all the welfare and staying on it for years and years and eating lobster while they take their drugs. The facts are that it's more often a white family and they are only on it for 6 months. Exactly what the program was put there to do, help people in temporary need. And yes there are some abusing the system. But aren't major corporations also abusing the system for even greater amounts money? Standard Oil needs a handout, really?

Chapter 12

Some Views on Free College

So for many years in America we had free college. Somehow we were able to afford it then? What happened? Now our middle class and poor start their lives in more debt than most of their parents every had (other than a mortgage on their home). Last year they had a vote to at least lower the interest rates on those loans and they couldn't even do that? We now have a government that is feeding off its own citizens. (See my chapter on, "We are seeing the End of Capitalism" chapter 29 for more on this).

When the manufacturing jobs were shipped out of the country, due to NAFTA, young people thought, "well I guess college is my only option." Besides the traditional colleges, all kinds of crappy schools came to the rescue, like Trump Academy. Most of them simply just ripped off their students, like Trump Academy, and there were not enough great jobs at the end of the line. One of my employees paid way too much at ITT Technical Institute before they folded. They only had one book in one class that everyone had to share. (Books were included in the price of the courses).

And I have to say that many of the guys that came to work for me at a minimum wage job, in my electronic repair store, took curriculums that there would never going to be that many jobs for, like recording engineer. One employee thought that after a one year long class in recording engineering, that someone was going to hand him control of the sound console at a rock concert? That's the dream that they sold them.

But it's good for our economy to have well trained people in the professions that need well trained people. It's an investment in the future. And we all know by now that if you have a good education, you're more likely to make more money, you'll probably not be in a gang or get your girl pregnant. And you're less likely to end up homeless or need food stamps or welfare. All things Born-Agains don't want, yet they don't want to pay for it either.

We're also seeing that students are choosing professions where they can make the most money, like business, because they have to be in a field that makes enough to pay back the student loan. That's horrible, because now some fields that don't pay enough will not have enough staff. Also, you will have people in fields that pay well, not because they have an interest in that field, but their just there for the money they can make.

And lastly, all these countries have free college. And some of them will even let foreigners and non-citizens go there and get their education for free too, imagine that!

Switzerland
France
Netherlands
Brazil
Slovenia
Greece
Germany
Finland.

When a Born-Again says, "We can't afford it," you can ask, "Why not, I thought you said we're the greatest country on Earth?" And by the way, why does the greatest country on Earth have to borrow money from China, a communist country to stay afloat?

Chapter 13

The Whole Problem of Immigration

Now of course, the Born-Again Republicans are in lock step on this issue too. **The** Trump administration officials, under pressure from the White House to provide a rationale for reducing the number of refugees allowed into the United States next year, rejected a study by the Department of Health and Human Services that found that refugees brought in $63 billion more in government revenues over the past decade than they cost us. They tried to hide the report because it went against their propaganda and racism.

Now, I'm not for open boarders either. But what Republicans like to ignore and never talk about is, the 1 million a year legal immigrants that were red carpeted into our country from wealthier and whiter countries for the last 20 years. People, who actually **do take our jobs** and some out bid us on buying homes.

Why did they let so many in? After they decimated our manufacturing jobs they said, "Oh crap, we fired our own customers what do we do now?" So they let rich people in to make up for it. But the Born-Again-Republican doesn't even know about this and doesn't care one bit. Even though there's now a migration of Natural born Americans from California to cheaper states where homes and rents are affordable.

The facts are, that illegal immigrants commit less crime because they do not want to be caught and then exported. They usually do not get free stuff for the same reason. They get free emergency room care because of a Republican, Reagan. However, do you know who does know how to use the system? The people from richer educated countries, it's not unusual for them to show up for food stamps in a brand new BMW.

The problem with letting people in from rich countries is this, they drive up real estate costs. Real estate people here have told me that even young people show up and pay cash for a home. In New York, Central Park goes dark at 3:00 PM now due to shadows from expensive high rises built for the very rich. And they have the power to get the government to ignore building coeds that were put there to prevent that kind of stuff.

Our first senior building in Burbank was full of Burbank seniors and is now devoted to people from one particular foreign country. I'm saying they broke the law or anything like that, but just pointing out that there are costs to us for all immigrations. I just think both types should be controlled because if housing and interstructure can't keep up, you're going to have serious problems. That may have contributed to our homeless problem. One good thing Trump actually did was cut down on the number of **legal** immigration too. Or did he?

The Statue of Concentration

Chapter 14

Arguments on DA Wall

Is the wall going to do any good? Is it worth the cost? Of course there should be a wall there and in many places it should be reinforced. It's already 350 miles long in the most problematic places. And you should know that the longer they make it, the more people die trying to get here through the desert or over the river. But it's not going to stop illegal immigration or drugs totally. It does make it harder though. But that wall will never extend from sea to shiny sea. And they already tunneled under it 50 times and all you need to get over it is a ladder or cherry picker. I even saw a video where three guys just took a long plastic pipe. One guy held on to one end as the other two pushed and he simply walks up the side of a building 3 stories high. So the wall is, really when you get down to it, just a symbol.

And drugs do not come in that way either, they come in right at the border. Now that we shipped our jobs to Mexico, there's a hug increase of trucks coming and going and it's very easy to hide drugs on them. So what they do need is more x-ray machines. And they are catching subs being towed behind boats. If they get spotted they release the cable to the sub and come get it later. But there's no reason you couldn't catapult the drugs over the wall or even use drones. One guy put some two by fours through the wall so kids to teeter totter and play with kids on the other side, so apparently you can just hand them through the wall as well. But they are sending tons of them, so trucking and subs are the preferred way to do it.

But the problem is also this, it ignores the millions of illegal's that just fly in and stay. E-verify would be a great solution. Every employer would have to verify if their new employees are here legally, at the very least they couldn't work here. Why is this not being widely used? Because many companies want cheaper labor. Meat packing was once a great paying job, not now. Taken over by many illegal's. So some corporations don't really want things to change all that much, including Trumps hotels.

But the bigger issue for me as I mentioned earlier is the 1 million **legal** immigrants they let in each year for over 20 years from rich countries. Those are the kinds of people likely to take your job because they are more educated. They're also likely to open a business in your field and be a competitor. They also really know how to milk the system.

Lastly as I write this there are photos on Facebook of Mexican kids climbing to the top of Trumps new wall, just for fun.

.

Chapter 15

The Reason We Should Have Some Regulations on Gun Ownership

I recently posted a question on a Facebook post that was about guns. The title of the post was "Give me one reason you need an AR-15" answer, "It's none of your @#&!ing business." I simply asked, "Where would you draw the line on what a person should be able to own, a handgun, hunting rifle, automatic machine gun, missile launcher, working tank, fully armed fighter jet or nuclear weapons." For most normal people they would say, hand guns or hunting rifles are OK but anything after that no. But no one would answer the question directly? But they sure did mention the 2nd amendment though, specially the part about, "A well regulated Militia, being necessary to the security of a free State." And they thought we need a well armed militia, because they fear our very own government may come for them and they'll have to fend them off. I kind of fear that too, but for me I fear the people in government that would do it, are the very people these guys keep voting for! (And that's happening, Trump, Lindsey Graham and Rubio, are now backing Red Flag laws, see end of this chapter).

So just to be clear, I asked a second time, "So you all think an American citizen should be able to have all those arms I mentioned, including nuclear weapons?" One friend of mine answered, "I believe your question has been answered now by a number of people William. Do you feel your question is not being duplicated?"

When anyone in government wants to ban assault rifles, the Born-Again hears, "Their coming for our guns." I mean really, that's what they actually hear, taking any gun away means taking all of them away, they think. If they did do that, what's next, pistols and hunting rifles of course, it's only logical, right? Again, they can't see things that are **different**.

But for years and years I heard that democrats are going to take away your guns. I think the Russians had a great time with this, because all you had to do is send a Facebook image to a gun owner showing, Obama or Hillary will take your guns away and for those people, that person was out for good. That button was hit heavy with Obama and did it happen, no? But this topic really gets people up at arms, literally.

When they bring up the 2nd amendment, you say, but we didn't have assault weapons when the constitution was written. We didn't have the ability to mow down 30 people in a few seconds either.

And when they bring up "A well regulated militia," remind them of the key words there, "**Well Regulated.**"
 But again this is just another one of those areas that they cannot see **differences**.

And they have no problem with Republicans in Washington that allowed people with mental problems to own guns. To most people, that seems to be a given. But Born-Agains, bowing to the gun industry, wanting to put a gun in everyone's hands, including teachers, got it past. But the Born-Again-Republican, won't even see how insane that policy is! Even back ground checks is going way too far for them. Because they're in fear of the government coming for them and their guns, because they'll know who has them. We have to pass a driver's test to get a driver's license because you're driving a dangerous vehicle down the street and can kill many people if you don't know how to drive right? But, when it comes to guns, they can't see that this is a **similar** issue.

As a last point, the gun industry loves it when there's a shooting because after each one more people go out and buy a gun to protect themselves and more ammo.

Side note update: This is going to be interesting. Trump, Lindsey Graham and Rubio, just today as I write this, are pushing Red Flag laws that really mean, anyone can point out a neighbour to the police who has guns and mention that they seem to be dangerous. Then the police can get just one judge, **with no trial**, to issue a warrant to confiscate their guns.

Quote; " *These Red Flag laws, properly known as Gun Confiscation Orders, are incompatible with actual due process and allow for the confiscation of firearms from innocent Americans," Erich Pratt, Gun Owners of America vice president, told the DCNF.*

So suddenly the tide has turned, the republicans are now the ones that are going to come for your guns, the people they voted for. I don't know how this will play out, but you can bet that the Republican Party is going to be losing a lot of votes from gun owners.

Chapter 16

What's Causing all these Shootings?

If you gather up all the data, video games, bad upbringing, a president spreading racists ideas, the internet, bad schooling and drugs, you'll find there is one common denominator. There is one thing most of them have in common and it's **psyche drugs**. It says right on the bottle and on every commercial that these drugs may cause **suicidal tendencies**. While most incidents just end in the person killing himself, some go out and kill others to, maybe for other reasons, like they are also racists or very troubled people. Being troubled is part of it, but the trigger is the psychic drug, at least 80% of them have that in common.

20 soldiers commit suicide every day and most of them have been put on these same drugs. They don't usually take others out with them, so the **troubled and/or racist** part is important. If you compare the graph of these incidents to the graph of these drugs being subscribed, they match pretty closely. These drugs are just handed out like candy. In some schools they had 30% of the kids on Ritalin. And they were subscribed for everything from fidgeting in class to unable to spell or read. But no one checked them for too much sugar for fidgeting in class. It was found in one school that no one had taught them how to read so the school psych just threw drugs at them. Have you seen the culinary services in American schools? Some have Coke machines in the hall ways.

I had an employee who told me that when he was in 6th grade, the kids would raid their parents medicine chest and bring their drugs to school and they'd exchange taking the drugs they found. He ended up hooked on cocaine when he worked for me and living in his van. I got him to Narconon that had a great sweat, sauna, vitamin program that worked. He finally, at the age of 26 got off drugs. Another friend also did the program because he couldn't remember being in grade school.

So why is this better known? Because the TV stations and radio stations make a fortune on drug commercials. It seems like every 5th commercial is for a drug for sleep, weight loss, or stopping smoking etc. They even have a drug to take if your current drug is not working well enough, so now you're on two of them. And they all say, "Let your doctor know if you're experiencing suicidal tendencies." Why do they even warn you? Because they know that many will and if they try to sue you, they can say, "Well we warned you. "

Why can't they make a drug that doesn't have dangerous side effects? This, by the way is, another gift from Crony Capitalism. Letting our citizens die so the gun manufactures and the drug companies can pick on our dead dying bones.

So if these drugs are causing the problem, then no one who's on them, should be allowed to own a gun. At least do that! But what does Trump do instead? He cancels a bill that Obama got past that said, "Mental patients should not be allowed to own a gun." Particularly young depressed males, the kind that make up most of our shooting events. Why not also pass a bill that hands them automatic weapons while you're at it?

Chapter 17

Is Trump a Racist?

It's amazing that the Born-Again's will actually suggest that Trump is <u>not a racist</u>. I mean, wow, now we're going to try and change the definition of words? I was asked recently why this Facebook photo was racist.

Bill board paid for by a gun shop and erected near that shop

It's because it plays on Trumps earlier racist comments for one thing. There are plenty of white democrats that don't like him, but does he pick on them though like this, telling them they should leave the country? Not to mention, how dangerous it is in these times, with the increase in racist attacks, to target people, specially a gun shop, that caters to some who may be dangerous gun nuts. But suggesting that people of color are not "really" American is a classic racist trope itself and one that is very much not new to Trump.

Then, Trump says recently, that democrats are the enemy. Couple that with the fact that these people have implants, this is a very dangerous situation and I sometimes wonder if Trump isn't really trying to knowingly or inadvertently start a race war.

The list of racist things he's done and said goes way back to his apartment building in the 70's where he was sued for not letting black people rent them. In his casino, anytime he was on the floor, they had to make all the black help leave the floor. And, you just listen to him talk about Mexico sending us rapists and drug dealers. He also suggested on his TV show "The Apprentice," that they have a show where blacks played against whites.

The other indicator is this, since he became president, racists violence has increased. From black churches being burned, Jewish grave yard head stones being over turned, shootings by people that clearly have been listening to him.

Now he didn't cause the racism, it's always been there. He just exposed it and showed us all that it's still there. But the worst thing he did is fan its flames and make bringing it out in the open OK again. Most people understand that his "Make America Great Again" slogan and hat, really means "Make America White Again." That line came from Ronald Reagan who was also a racist. Do you remember Willy Horton who he made a poster criminal child for his campaign? Willy go out of jail then murdered someone. There were plenty of other races that he could have used, but it was no accident that he picked a black man. It was a message to his base.

Yes, this area really shows how delusional they can be. Someone posted the question on Facebook. "Is Trump a racists?" Now, to even have to ask that question tells you a lot more about the mind of a Trump supporter then you may want to know. But after numerous posts saying that he is not a racist, the person who posted the question then boldly asked, "For those of you who said "yes", what are you basing your answer on? Just curious. Or is it simply that he is not liberal so he must be racist? By the way that statement was made by a Born Again Christian.

So I posted the list below showing some 38 times he did a racists act or made a racist statement. After reading that very long list, one Trump supporter commented, **"None of the things you listed are anywhere close to acts of racism."**

Then he added, "Look up Dr. Alveda King and Medgar Evers. His brother is a Trump supporter." As if that proves anything. There are many people of other races and even woman who also support Trump, that's just more proof of them being delusional than a proof that he's not a racist.

But let's look at the definitions of these words for further clarification.

Racist;

Showing or feeling discrimination or prejudice against people of other races, or believing that a particular race is superior to another.
"We are investigating complaints about racist abuse at the club"
Is the belief in the superiority of one race over another. It may also include prejudice, discrimination, or antagonism directed against other people.

Now, the very first thing that shows up on that list is a court case that he lost when it was found he was refusing to rent to black people. That clearly is **Racial Discrimination.**

Another example,
Speaking about immigration in a bipartisan meeting in January 2018, Trump **reportedly asked**, in reference to Haiti and African countries, "Why are we having all these people from shithole countries come here?" He then reportedly suggested that the US should take more people from countries like Norway. The implication: Immigrants from predominantly <u>white</u> countries are good, while immigrants from predominantly <u>black</u> countries are bad.

Here he points to "darker" countries and makes the statement why are they coming, then says we want people from these "whiter" countries instead. Clearly exhibiting the feeling of one race is **superior** to another, (see definition again.)

Now, the reason the Born-Again can't see this is they are **delusional** on this subject. They cannot see it because of the implant when it should be clear to them because it's clear to everyone else. But let's look up **delusional** and see if it applies?

Delusional;
Believing something to be true that is clearly not. Someone who is not thinking clearly. Used to describe someone attached to an idea which is obviously false.

Even if you show them or read the definition of racist to them, they still won't be able to see it. Again, it's as if they have been hypnotized to not be able to converse clearly on this subject. They cannot have a *rational* argument on this subject. So, don't waste time on them, but do make your case for others that are rational who may be listening in.

Now there is one other point on his racism. I just heard there is a new book coming out that the author discovered about Trump. He wrote that his racism has become a useful tool for him.

If you pay attention to the news, you can see it for yourself. Whenever something happens that incriminates him, he makes a racial statement to take attention off that subject. So, in July of 2019, his good friend Epstein is indicted and thrown in jail for having a sex ring of under aged teenagers. And many other public officials are implicated, including him. What does he do? He tweets the following statement about the tribe;

Trump;
So interesting to see "Progressive" Democrat Congresswomen, who originally came from countries whose governments are a complete and total catastrophe, the worst, most corrupt and inept anywhere in the world (if they even have a functioning government at all), now loudly......
... and viciously telling the people of the United States, the greatest and most powerful Nation on earth, how our government is to be run. Why don't they go back and help fix the totally broken and crime infested places from which they came. Then come back and show us how....
.... is done. These places need your help badly, you can't leave fast enough. I'm sure that Nancy Pelosi would be very happy to quickly work out free travel arrangements!

Now, because his base is highly racists as well, all the attention goes off the more serious subject, that he might be implicated in having participated in the sex ring, to these four woman Reps. Alexandria Ocasio-Cortez (D-NY), Ayanna Pressley (D-MA), Ilhan Omar (D-MN), and Rashida Tlaib (D-MI).

He doesn't care that his statement is inaccurate, that they came from another country, when three of them were born right here and even AOC was born his city? Because it has the effect he wants, it takes the attention off of "his" situation. The fact that it's inaccurate means it will be discussed even **more often**! That makes it work even better in his eyes. This in no way means he is not a racist, but simply points out how he uses racism for his own purposes.

This is **not** a complete list of his racist remarks and actions. I'm sure there will be more before I finish this book. Trump has a long history of racist controversies,

(From a VOX article 2016)
Here's a breakdown of Trump's history, taken largely from **Dara Lind's list for Vox** and an **op-ed by Nicholas Kristof in the New York Times**:

> **1973:** The US Department of Justice — under the Nixon administration, out of all administrations — **sued** the Trump Management Corporation for violating the Fair Housing Act. Federal officials found **evidence** that Trump had refused to rent to black tenants and lied to black applicants about whether apartments were available, among other accusations. Trump said the federal government was trying to get him to rent to welfare recipients. In the aftermath, he signed an agreement in 1975 agreeing not to discriminate to renters of color without admitting to discriminating before.

> **1980s:** Kip Brown, a former employee at Trump's Castle, accused another one of Trump's businesses of discrimination. "When Donald and Ivana came to the casino, the bosses would order all the black people off the floor," Brown **said**. "It was the eighties, I was a teenager, but I remember it: They put us all in the back. "

> **1988:** In a commencement speech at Lehigh University, Trump **spent much of his speech** accusing countries like Japan of "stripping the United States of economic dignity. " This matches much of his current rhetoric on China.

1989: In a controversial case that's been characterized as a modern-day lynching, four black teenagers and one Latino teenager — the "Central Park Five" — were accused of attacking and raping a jogger in New York City. Trump immediately took charge in the case, running **an ad in local papers** demanding, "BRING BACK THE DEATH PENALTY. BRING BACK OUR POLICE!" The teens' convictions were later vacated after they spent **seven to 13 years in prison**, and the city paid $41 million in a settlement to the teens. But Trump in October 2016 **said** he still believes they're guilty, despite the DNA evidence to the contrary.

1991: A **book** by John O'Donnell, former president of Trump Plaza Hotel and Casino in Atlantic City, quoted Trump's criticism of a black accountant: "Black guys counting my money! I hate it. The only kind of people I want counting my money are short guys that wear yarmulkes every day. ... I think that the guy is lazy. And it's probably not his fault, because laziness is a trait in blacks. It really is, I believe that. It's not anything they can control. " Trump at first denied the remarks, but later said in **a 1997 Playboy interview** that "the stuff O'Donnell wrote about me is probably true. "

1992: The Trump Plaza Hotel and Casino **had to pay a $200,000 fine** because it transferred black and women dealers off tables to accommodate a big-time gambler's prejudices.

1993: In congressional testimony, Trump **said** that some Native American reservations operating casinos shouldn't be allowed because "they don't look like Indians to me. "

2000: In opposition to a casino proposed by the St. Regis Mohawk tribe, which he saw as a financial threat to his casinos in Atlantic City, Trump secretly ran a **series of ads** suggesting the tribe had a "record of criminal activity [that] is well documented. "

2004: In season two of THE APPRENTICE, Trump **fired** Kevin Allen, a black contestant, for being overeducated. "You're an unbelievably talented guy in terms of education, and you haven't done anything," Trump said on the show. "At some point you have to say, 'That's enough. '"

2005: Trump **publicly pitched** what was essentially THE APPRENTICE: WHITE PEOPLE VS. BLACK PEOPLE. He **said** he "wasn't particularly happy" with the most recent season of his show, so he was considering "an idea that is fairly controversial — creating a team of successful African Americans versus a team of successful whites. Whether people like that idea or not, it is somewhat reflective of our very vicious world. "

2010: In 2010, there was a huge national controversy over the "Ground Zero Mosque" — a proposal to build a Muslim community center in Lower Manhattan, near the site of the 9/11 attacks. Trump opposed the project, calling it "insensitive," and **offered to buy out** one of the investors in the project. On THE LATE SHOW WITH DAVID LETTERMAN, Trump **argued**, referring to Muslims, "Well, somebody's blowing us up. Somebody's blowing up buildings, and somebody's doing lots of bad stuff. "

2011: Trump played a **big role** in pushing false rumors that Obama — the country's first black president — was not born in the US. He even sent investigators to Hawaii to **look into Obama's birth certificate**. Obama later released his birth certificate, calling Trump a **"carnival barker. "** (The **research** has found a strong correlation between "birtherism," as this conspiracy theory is called, and racism.) Trump has **reportedly continued** pushing this conspiracy theory in private.

2011: While Trump suggested that Obama wasn't born in the US, he also argued that maybe Obama wasn't a good enough student to have gotten into Columbia or Harvard Law School, and demanded Obama release his university transcripts. Trump **claimed**, "I heard he was a terrible student. Terrible. How does a bad student go to Columbia and then to Harvard?"

As a candidate and president, Trump has made many more racist comments

Trump launched his campaign in 2015 by **calling** Mexican immigrants "rapists" who are "bringing crime" and "bringing drugs" to the US. His campaign was largely built on building a wall to keep these immigrants out of the US.

As a candidate in 2015, Trump **called** for a ban on all Muslims coming into the US. His administration eventually implemented a **significantly watered-down version of the policy**.

When asked at a 2016 Republican debate whether all 1. 6 Million hate the US, Trump **said**, "I mean a lot of them. I mean a lot of them. "

He **argued** in 2016 that Judge Gonzalo Curiel — who was overseeing **the Trump University lawsuit** — should recues himself from the case because of his Mexican heritage and membership in a Latino lawyers association. House Speaker Paul Ryan, who endorsed Trump, later **called** such comments "the textbook definition of a racist comment. "

Trump has been **repeatedly slow** to condemn white supremacists who endorse him, and he **regularly re-tweeted** messages from white supremacists and neo-Nazis during his presidential campaign.

He **tweeted and later deleted** an image that showed Hillary Clinton in front of a pile of money and by a Jewish Star of David that said, "Most Corrupt Candidate Ever!" The tweet had some very obvious anti-Semitic imagery, but Trump **insisted** that the star was a sheriff's badge, and **said** his campaign shouldn't have deleted it.

Trump has **repeatedly referred** to Sen. Elizabeth Warren (D-MA) as "Pocahontas," using her controversial — and **later walked-back** — claims to Native American heritage as a punch line.

At the 2016 Republican convention, Trump officially seized the mantle of **the "law and order" candidate** — an obvious **dog whistle** playing to white fears of black crime, even though crime in the US is **historically low**. His **speeches, comments, and executive actions** after he took office have continued this line of messaging.

In **a pitch to black voters** in 2016, Trump **said**, "You're living in poverty, your schools are no good, you have no jobs, 58 percent of your youth is unemployed. What the hell do you have to lose?"

Trump **stereotyped** a black reporter at a press conference in February 2017. When April Ryan asked him if he plans to meet and work with the Congressional Black Caucus, he repeatedly asked her to set up the meeting — even as she insisted that she's "just a reporter. "

In the week after **white supremacist protests in Charlottesville, Virginia**, in August 2017, Trump **repeatedly said** that "many sides" and "both sides" were to blame for the violence and chaos that ensued — suggesting that the white supremacist protesters were morally equivalent to counter protesters that stood against racism. He also said that there were "some very fine people" among the white supremacists. All of this seemed like a dog whistle to white supremacists — and many of them took it as one, with white nationalist Richard Spencer **praising** Trump for "defending the truth. "

Throughout 2017, Trump **repeatedly attacked** NFL players who, by kneeling or otherwise silently protesting during the national anthem, demonstrated against systemic racism in America.

Trump **reportedly said** in 2017 that people who came to the US from Haiti "all have AIDS," and he lamented that people who came to the US from Nigeria would never "go back to their huts" once they saw America. The White House **denied** that Trump ever made these comments.

Speaking about immigration in a bipartisan meeting in January 2018, Trump **reportedly asked**, in reference to Haiti and African countries, "Why are we having all these people from shithole countries come here?" He then reportedly suggested that the US should take more people from countries like Norway. The implication: Immigrants from predominantly white countries are good, while immigrants from predominantly black countries are bad.

Trump **denied** making the "shithole" comments, although some senators present at the meeting **said** they happened. The White House, meanwhile, **suggested** that the comments, like Trump's remarks about the NFL protests, will play well to his base.

The only connection between Trump's remarks about the NFL protests and his "shithole" comments is race.

Trump mocked Elizabeth Warren's presidential campaign, again calling her "Pocahontas" in a **tweet** before adding, "See you on the campaign TRAIL, Liz!" The capitalized "TRAIL" is **seemingly a reference** to the Trail of Tears — a horrific act of ethnic cleansing in the 19th century in which Native Americans were forcibly relocated, causing thousands of deaths.

Trump **tweeted** that several black and brown members of Congress — Reps. Alexandria Ocasio-Cortez (D-NY), Ayanna Pressley (D-MA), Ilhan Omar (D-MN), and Rashida Tlaib (D-MI) — are "from countries whose governments are a complete and total catastrophe" and that they should "go back" to those countries. It's a common racist trope to say that black and brown people, particularly immigrants, should go back to their countries of origin. Three of four of the members of Congress whom Trump targeted were born in the US.

Chapter 18

The Problems and Advantages of Tariffs

For many years the USA had tariffs on many products that were being imported. And those tariffs were there to protect our companies and our work force. A country like China that pays its employees .50 cents an hour can make a product so cheap, they could put an American manufacture out of business. Even food crops could be financed by the government, and they are, and they can use prison labor too. That's why tariffs were there to protect us and our businesses.

They did, till our corporations got the government to get rid of most of them. Why would they do that? Because they realized they could move the whole factory out of the country and use that cheap government controlled forced labor. Using American workers means you have to pay over time, vacations, holidays off, medical etc. All the good stuff we fought for with sometimes, our very lives. I mean we are just so needy. But the tariffs prevented them from doing this years ago, because when the product came back in, it would cost more due to the tariffs. So the company would lose the benefit of cheaper labor. **Ingenious wasn't it?**

The corporations got the government to get rid of the tariffs in the name of **FREE TRADE!** But what it was really about was getting rid of **good high paying jobs** in the USA and sending them elsewhere, so the corporations could make a fortune. So millions of good paying manufacturing jobs left the country. Ross Perot warned us that if these trade deals went through, we would hear a giant sucking sound. And he was right, that is exactly what happened.

The government lost all that income tax income from all those millions of good paying lost jobs too. What did all those people do? Well, if you were young enough, you could go back to college and get a better job, maybe. My sister worked for the gas company and was high enough up the ladder that when they shipped her job away, she had benefits she could live on. She always wanted to be a school teacher so she went back to college. But it was not to be, she was actually too old to be a teacher and she was running out of retirement funds, so she stopped. The banking failures of the 2008's took away a lot more of her retirement package.

But many other factory workers just went to low paying Wallmart food services jobs. They tried to retrain autoworkers for McDonalds but they couldn't work fast enough. For more on this and how it destroyed Detroit, watch "Roger and Me" by Michael Moore, that movie tells the whole sad story.
By the way, the reason labor got screwed was that when they got together to do NAFTA and the other trade agreements too, labor was not invited to the table. Why? Because labor was the main course. That's what they would be feasting on.

Now Trump was right, we don't have fair trade agreements with many countries. But will his tariffs work? He might get China to budge a little, but it's not going to bring any major manufacturing plants back home. Why? Because they plan ahead, sometimes ten or 20 years ahead. They don't have any confidence that he will stay in office long enough to trust the process. He probably will not be re-elected and may not even finish his term considering what's going on. So no major corporation is going to trust him and ship any factory back home. And why should they anyway? They'll have to go from $5. 00 a day to a minimum of $15. 00 or more an hour with benefits? Why would you do that?

And of course China has always put tariffs on our products coming in to them, which means our companies that are selling to them now lose sales too.

That's really what Trump is complaining about. How did they every agree to that? They keep their tariffs on us and we have to get rid of ours on them? But they did it anyway, because it wasn't about **fair trade**, although sure they would like that too, it was really about getting rid of **high paying American jobs**, that was the golden ring that they wanted and they got.

But because of Trumps tariffs, the worst part is this, China may find other countries to buy those items from and many companies may permanently lose them as a customer.

Who pays the tariff? We pay the tariff. The product that comes in cost the American supplier 30% more or whatever rate Trump puts on that product. That cost gets passed on to us the buyer I.E. you and me.

One last thing that could be done instead of a tariff is this, lower the amount of goods China can export to us. That way it **does** penalize them. The price would still go up here because of less supply. But at least they would be penalized.

The fact is, there is probably much better ways to effect a change then going about it like a bull in a china shop. A much better way to run any government is this, you find the best people who know the most about the subject in question and then do that.

Bill Moyers used to have a great TV show where he did just that. Man, he found people who really new what they were talking about. 60 Minuets often does that as well, but the best source I found today is on Pacifica Radio. "Back Ground Briefing" with Ion Masters, for instance, 4 days a week and Sunday, he interviews 3 people per show, that worked for the state department, or the justice department, or work in congress. Many have written detailed books that dive deeply into these various subjects that they are experts in.

There are many other shows too on that station, that interview people who are in the know. All their shows can be heard anytime on line.

NPR by the way, used to do this kind of reporting too. But since they gave up on only public funding and now have commercials, they can't dive as deeply into subjects that might step on the toes of their new corporate sponsors. You may recall how even 60 Minutes was almost shut down when they were going to do a story about the tobacco industry intentionally suppressing the dangers of their product. Why? Because they were partly financed or owned by the tobacco industry. And notice now, how all the other similar shows. 20/20, used to do investigative reporting and now, they just review court cases.

You might even say this about these people **in the know**, if they're **not** invited to Fox news, they probably know what they're talking about. You could also say that about the main stream media as well. Some of them know their subjects so well that the mainstream media wouldn't air them either, because main stream media is also in bed with the corporations. A lot of these kinds of problems seem to end up being caused by the major corporations.

So that's the best way to handle government problems. Find the best people you can and do that! But that's not in Trumps cards, his personality doesn't work that way. Lots of others don't either because that's not what they're there for to make things better for all of us. They're there, and were elected, to make things better for the people that **financed their campaigns**. If we get some crumbs in the process, that's entirely by accident or by court order. You know it's been said that the "Trickle Down Theory," for instance, was actually rich people peeing on us.

Chapter 19

The Disadvantages of Privatizing

What is privatizing all about? Well mostly Republicans want to have private industry get paid for schools, prisons, making the food for our soldiers, the post office and anything else they can ripe us off on. There is a ton of money to be had and they want it to go to them. Halliburton is making a fortune on feeding our soldiers and doing other services the Pentagon used to take care of. In the past the soldiers did all that themselves, I know, because my dad was a cook in the army in world war ll.

But it's really about diverting billions from the government to private companies. As one example, a report from congressional Democrats said Halliburton charged the government $2. 68 per gallon to import gasoline to **Iraq** from Kuwait, but a government agency did the same work for $1.57 a gallon. That difference had cost the government an extra $166.5 million, the report said. It's pretty obvious it will cost more because, like healthcare, they're going to take a profit right off the top. And you're going to get less service. If they privatize the post office, you can say good by to mail 6 days a week and the price is likely to skyrocket too. Private prisons are being scrutinized for lack of prisoner care. Like the healthcare insurance companies, they make more money if they deny care.

Governor Snyder of Michigan declared three of the poorest, mostly black districts into an emergency zone? Which got rid of their local Mayors and then he replaced them with his chosen people who had complete control of those districts.

The water was switched because Snyder wanted to replace the perfectly good pipe line from Lake Huron, glassier water, to his pipe line that he and his friends would own and charge the city for, in others words privatize it. To pull that off they had to turn off the older pipeline while they built theirs. But all I heard on the news was, they did it to save money.

The Charter school issue, that Betsy DeVos is so anxious to implement, really means that money is taken away from public schools to pay for private schools.

They want public schools to do a bad job so they can say, Charter schools are better. They have been criticized for taking the best students (and also often the whiter students) and because class sizes can be smaller, they can do better. But that does not always happen either.

But money to pay for them is taken from public schools, so they have less money and get defunded in the process. Which is what the proponents or this want to happen. The worse they get the more likely people will want privately run charter schools.

School of Hard Knots

Chapter 20

The Voter Photo Id Argument

This is really about making it difficult for poorer people to vote. There really isn't a lot of people voting over and over again, it's been studied ad nauseam, but there sure are people being dropped or prevented from being allowed to vote. A report just came out showing 17 million Americans were purged from voter rolls between 2016 and 2018. This has been done by both parties, currently more by Republicans. The Born-Again has no empathy for poor people and the hassle it can be for them to get a photo ID.

They may have to leave work, spend a day going to another city, paying fees to get their original birth certificate, then take that to the DMV that also may be in another city and get verified. That's exactly what I had to do, because I needed to get a passport and I didn't know that over my whole life, like Obama, I only had a copy of my birth certificate. I needed the original. I had to take off work and drive to Anaheim from Burbank? Stand in a line that came out the door and out to the street. After paying some fees I could drive back home. Then I had to take off work again, stand in another line, to get my passport. Poor people can't afford to do all that! Living paycheck to paycheck on a Wallmart or Taco Bell paycheck means you're probably not going to be voting.

But the real fraud in voter suppression is committed by many governors and public officials in many states like Florida. Thousands of voters were purged because their name was similar to someone else's name that was registered in another state. Any excuse they can find. This was of course only applied to Democrat voters.

But even in more liberal states, like California, you can be purged if your name is too strange like Mohammed, or Garcia. They don't enter ½ of the paper voter entries. They already have your name in the computer why do you need to fill out a paper entry that someone might not be able to read?

Then there were the voting machines that already had 2000 votes for Bush before the polls opened. And right now many states, including California, have purchased, at great expense, new voting machines that have no paper trail or any other way to verify the results. And they are all easily hackable. Paper ballots are the cheapest way to go. Why not do that?

In many states you can vote by absentee ballot. You now have a paper trail and you don't have to leave work to vote, you can take your time. And in California you can actually check to see if your vote was counted on line. And in many states you can make sure that you have not been purged. You should check this well before every election.

Chapter 21

People on Welfare Should all be Drug Tested

The spin doctors keep pumping this idea out because it's a technique. You blame one group of people, make them the enemy, so they don't notice who really is ripping them off. The fact is, whenever they have done drug testing for people on welfare, they find out that it costs them more money to do the testing than they save by finding people on drugs. So it's not cost effective to do it.

But I always say, how about we test the major corporations CEO's and leading stock holders for drugs, because they're also getting government handouts in the form or huge tax breaks and subsidies. But the Born-Again doesn't care about rich people taking handouts. Only poor people shouldn't get free stuff. And they are happy to shower rich people with more cash even if they have to pay higher taxes and lose government programs to do it. They cannot see how this is a **similar** issue.

Will Rogers ones said, "A Republican is a person who never enjoyed a meal unless he knew someone else was starving." That seems to apply here.

The difference between a conservative and a liberal is this. If they find corruption in say food stamps, 1 out of 7 people cheated, conservatives would shut it all down because of the cheats. But a liberal would ignore it and try and fix it, so that the six people that didn't cheat still get taken care of. If you sum up the difference between a liberal or a conservative with one word, it would be liberals seem to have **Empathy.**

Chapter 22

A Discussion about Golf Trips and Benghazi

Now these two are very interesting and really pushes on the idea of unable to see **similarities**. Because if you recall all the clamor about Obama's golf trips, you see how crazy this is. Obama played golf 304 times in 8 years. At the current rate, Trump is estimated to play 628 times in 8 years. I think Obama also played too much golf too, that's a lot of golfing, but is it just partisan politics that they don't say anything about the person who is playing twice as much golf? How is it no longer a problem? Same thing with the national debt, used to be a problem, not anymore, not when they have the purse strings.

But on the subject of Benghazi, after 4 Republican led investigations they found nothing. 6 to 7 Million dollars wasted. Yeah, Hillary dumped her phone data and connived to make sure Bernie didn't get in was far worse, **that's what they should have locked her up for**. But they're still bringing up Benghazi? When they do I always say, Gesundheit.

But what they never point out is this, before the incident, Republicans voted to reduce spending on embassy security! Now, I'm no fan of Hillary or her husband who gave us NAFTA. But when I try to give a Born-Again-Republican talking points and mention how Hillary, being the good corporate democrat that she is, was all fine with making sure we didn't know what food Monsanto was putting their GMOs in, they don't care about that. Their news source, of course, is not going to mention that tidbit so it doesn't exist for them. And there's the tidbit too, that I like to mention on Obama who, like Bush Jr. also made a deal with the drug companies to not get them to lower their prices for Obama care. Obama was just another **Corporate Democrat** too, although a lot better than most Republican presidents I recall.

Chapter 23

Arguments for Smaller Government

Now, often anytime you suggest something that might help some problem their battle cry is usually "Smaller Government." But they have no problem having bigger government when it comes to something they want, like drug testing people on welfare, or increasing the pentagon budget. They have swallowed this pill from the Republican party. But when you examine what the Republican party is doing is really nothing to do with smaller government and all to do with taking money from the poor and middle class programs and handing it to the very rich. They have no problem raising the national debt when ever they're in charge.

They align themselves a bit with the Libertarian Party on this issue. I used to be a Libertarian, till I realized, that the biggest plank in their party is "**free trade**." They think that if you have "**free trade**" everything will fix itself. Because the guy with the best price or product will win and the losers will not succeed and thus we all benefit. I went along with this till I realized **you cannot have free trade when you already have huge monopolies already controlling things!** Just try to open up an oil refinery and see how far you get with a better price on gasoline. In California there was one independent refinery at one time. And whenever the big guys started gouging us on gas, this refinery would help control the price, and help keep it lower.

Free trade is actually true and workable, **but not if there are hug monopolies around.** I'm not sure why that refinery closed but of all people, reverend Pat Robinson, tried to reopen it. But when he tried to get a loan from the bank, Standard Oil told the bank that if they gave him a loan they would be pulling all their money out.

While on the subject of monopolies. When I was in school in the 60's, I recall studying monopolies and how bad they were for the reason just stated. So what happened? Due to crony Capitalism, huge corporations have been allowed to grow and that is a very bad thing for us because of so little competition. Diamonds for instance are really not that rare in the world, but one company, De Beers controls all the diamond mines and suppliers in the whole world, even in Russia. Because if some country tried to unload them on a **Free Market**, the price would drop. Just like that refinery in California, keep it closed. Sun glasses are also controlled too. One company runs the whole show. That's why you pay more. Just the opposite of **free trade**. GE developed a machine that could make the best grade of diamonds that was never used. Probably visited by De Beers

And did you know that all these CEOs of these corporations sit on each other's board of directors? Talk about a conflict of interest. What small start up is going to be invited to sit at those tables?

Foot note: *As a vertically integrated company, Luxottica designs, manufactures, distributes and retails its **eyewear** brands, including LensCrafters, Sunglass Hut, Apex by Sunglass Hut, Pearle Vision, Sears Optical, Target Optical, Eyemed vision care plan, and **Glasses**. com. Its best known brands are Ray-Ban, Persol, and Oakley.*

Chapter 24

Is there Really "Fake News"?

Yes, there certainly is fake news, but it's not the news that Trump thinks it is. He of course has to discount any bad news about his numerous mistakes and blunders, so the best way to cover all that up is tell his base, it's just fake news. But what he probably does not know is this, since most of the major news sources are owned by only 6 corporations, they decide what we get to hear and more importantly, don't hear. Did you know that the story about us helping the Saudis starving woman, children, babies and men in Yemen was suppressed by the major news services, including CNN (until recently)? Many newspapers covered it though, but who reads newspapers anymore? Pacifica Radio covered it, that's how I found out.

Did you know that the distract managers in West Virginia when they turned in the numbers for the primary with Bernie and Hillary all lied accept for one? Bernie won all 55 districts but all but one of the delegates decided to go with Hillary instead. In Michael Moor's latest movie, Fereinhiet 11-9 you can see delegates with tape over their mouths that said "Silenced" and a sign one of them held that said, "Bernie won all 55 counties."

And did you know the lead in the water in Flint Michigan, the governor knew about for over a year and a half. He new the water was poisoned? And the people doing the blood tests for high levels of lead, were asked to fudge the numbers.

And when Obama visited the people of flint thought, "Now will get some action." But the corporate president Obama, simple sipped some Flint water, gave two speeches and then did absolutely nothing.

And when Trump came down that escalator with his wife to announce he was running for president, did you know that it was just made up? He paid people to be there and it was just really a stunt to get NBC to pay him more for his TV show. But after making his racist remarks, NBC fired him instead. But since so many real supports liked the idea, he decided to run, probably to milk if for all he could, never realizing that he might win.

So where was our news services then? You have news that is being suppressed by the so called "Liberal Media" and you have the rest of the news being ignored or spun by the "Conservative Media."

Here is some data to consider, There are 2,570: Hours of conservative talk broadcasts each day. Versus, 254: Hours of progressive talk broadcast each day. Maybe if there were more hours of progressive shows, we'd have more Born-Again-Democrats?

And you can bet that those conservative stations where not telling their people all about Obama's great employment numbers.

During the Vietnam War, which even defense sectary McNamara now said, really had no purpose, kept that data quite. The major news services promoted the war. That is, till one very popular newscaster of the time stepped up to the plate, Walter Cronkite and pronounced the War a 'Stalemate.' But more important started showing the real costs of that war and showing our kids coming home in body bags. Then everything changed and the peace movement began.

Right now Facebook and others use algorithms to let you know what is going on. A news story about climate warming might be sent to you, who may be concerned about that but they may send something very different to someone with a different opinion about it. So don't think everyone is seeing the same posts that you see.

But realize this, besides not reporting a story at all, all news sources have the power to decide what's important and what isn't. I know of one church that was repeatedly investigated by the IRS. The story would appear on the front pages of the L.A. Times and when nothing was found the story saying, nothing was found, would be printed on the back pages. That's one way a newspaper controls the news. They can say, "Well we printed that nothing was found." But it was on the back page.

Where something appears in a newspaper or a newscast, is important. And if you look at most of the news sources, the biggest stories are on the front page or the first story, if it's a TV news show. And often the leading story has a transgression by a celebrity or politician that involves stealing money or sexual impropriety. I even did a sculpture on this subject called, "The Media Feeding Frenzy."

When they get a story like this you can almost see them drooling, like their feasting on a great aged finely barbequed piece of meat.

And no surprise that the one news source that always comes in last when "truth in news stories" is analyzed, is Fox. The one news source that our president watches constantly. And how bazaar that one of the news caster on that show would be having daily conversations with the president? How can a news source be taken seriously, when one of their key reporters, (and I use that term loosely) is in bed with the person he's reporting on?

And we have also seen that news source influencing the presidents decisions. Just look at what happened over the government shut down over the wall.

The president's propagandists were having a great time. Portions of the government shuttered and hundreds of thousands of federal employees would have to work without pay for weeks, Fox's airwaves were **filled with hoorays for the president and congratulations for him to remain firm**. The hosts didn't mention Trump's possible political troubles over this, to the contrary, they urged the rest of his party to stick with him regardless of the consequences. "If this takes 150 days, I think the Republican Party needs to stand united with the president," argued Sean Hannity.

So the tail is wagging the dog now? And who owns this news service, Murdock, a guy from Australia, a foreigner, now a citizen, who became one so he could operate in the USA. To refresh your memory, he's the same guy who owned the Tabloid Newspaper, "News of the World" that lasted 168 years, that is, till Murdock and his clan got hold of it and got caught illegally wire tapping peoples cell phones. It is no more.

These are now the seedy characters that have direct access to our president. Who are working towards complete control of our government via the Republican Party and corporate Democrats. And were worried about the Russians? They would love to have the control that Murdock has.

Then there's, MSNBC that is supposed to be a liberal news source? Really? Then why was Chris Mathews condemning Single Payer? Why do they support the more Corporate Democrat candidates and play down the progressives?

The free press has always been seen as the fourth department in our government. Our government was set up to be checks and balances of the three branches. But the press was to be the outside source to help keep things known and in balance. And now we see the press cozying up to one branch of our government, the president and corporate interests. How can you believe that what they're reporting isn't anything but fake news?

So to really find out what's going on, realize the main stream media cannot be trusted fully either. So you won't be seeing me being interviewed on CNN or MSNBC and certainly not Fox. So seek out shows and books that are usually not being talked about on these programs. In the last appendix 5, I listed TV programs, radio shows, movies and books that I've found the most accurate and enlightened. Many of the shows and books I mention have no problem complaining about both parties, which is a good **indicator of truthfulness**.

Most of the authors I mentioned there will never be interviewed on the main stream media and that's how they control things, just don't mention it.

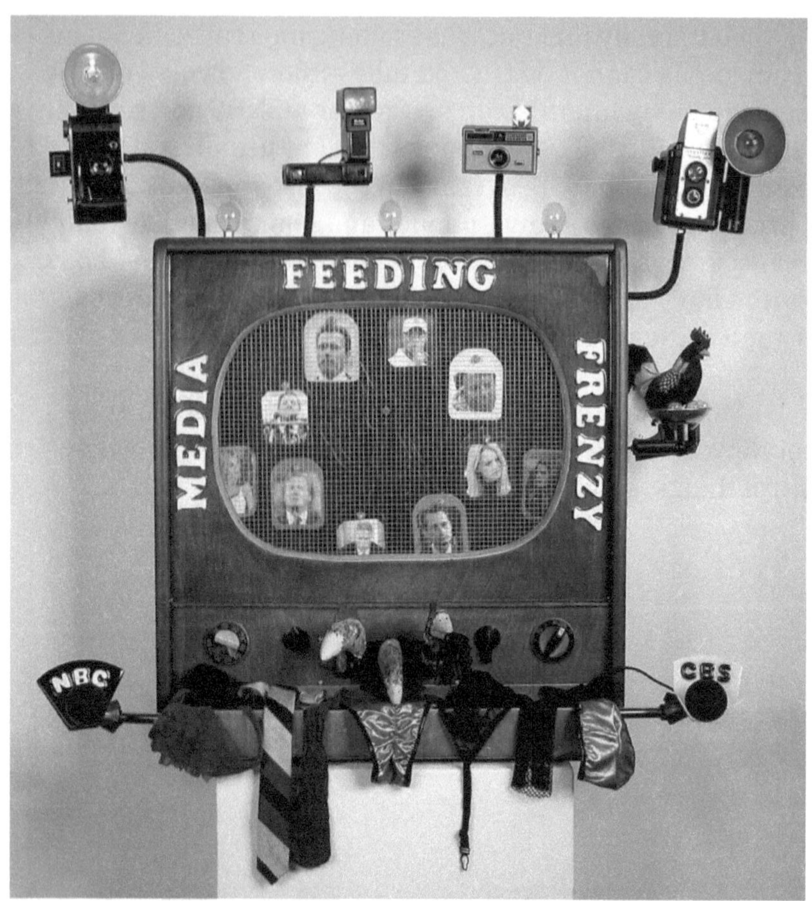

The Media Feeding Frenzy

Chapter 25

Is there Really Climate Change
that's Caused by Man?

Now, here we go again, is there climate change caused by man? Wow, how can anyone deny this? We Pump tons and tons of crap in the air every single day worldwide. What did they think would happen? They pumped so much corporate waste into the rivers that some caught fire. People have shown videos of their tap water catching fire!

But, like the fact that most shootings are done by people on Physic drugs, this one is also suppressed for the very same reasons. Many companies would go under or lose money if we all knew that our factories where killing us and the world. Most of them paying out millions to our so called "News Services" (in the form of paid commercials) to keep this all quiet. So, no wonder it's not better known. But to the born again it's even worse. They listen to corporate TV and radio exclusively who are all totally controlled and financed by corporations who are making a profit on having things stay **exactly as they are**. All screwed up. Where is our main stream Walter Cronkite on this issue?

So let's look at the facts. Scientists can't be trusted? Really? I bet when they need medical help they have faith in science. But we don't even need scientist to understand this. Just look at the graphs, the graphs that scientist use to figure things out.

If you compare the graph of oceans rising and global temperatures rising, with the graph of the tons and tones of crap that gets pumped into the air every single day around the world, what do you see? They match up! That's something called, "Date coincident." On this date we had and increase in this and then on that same period, we had an increase in something else. The chickens were only laying 156 eggs a day. A new roaster is introduced and suddenly, the eggs go up to 285 eggs a day, thanks Cluck Norris!

That's date coincident. Who done it, what done it? But the born again will not get that either. And it's true that it could just be a "coincident" and nothing at all about dumping billions of tons of carbon into the air. But here are some actual facts.

- Each and every second 310 Kg of toxic chemicals are released into our air, land, and water by industrial facilities around the world.

- This amounts to approximately **10 million tons (over 21 billion pounds)** of toxic chemicals released into our environment by industries each year.

That message was brought to you by Ralphs, Pretty good Grocer or at least that's what the ad said next to it. But really, it was compiled by, U.S. Environmental Protection Agency (EPA) Which means it will be soon suppressed and removed from public view.

I just today, had a discussion about this with some Born-Again's and one said, "There's a NASA study that showed hydrocarbons are actually cooling the planet." Before I had a chance to check that claim out, the post was gone. To the contrary every NASA post that I found said that hydrocarbons are increasing global warming.

Now there could be factors like the changing of the magnetic field of Earth.

That is happening and could be contributing to the problem but if so, all the more reason to cut down on emissions. And remember when the ozone layer was being destroyed by chlorofluorocarbons (CFCs) and halons—gases formerly found in aerosol spray cans and refrigerants? Well, we did something about it and that's not a problem now. Science worked then didn't it?

But the whole discounting of science is part of the troupe. Corporations who are making money off old dirty polluting technologies, want to continue making money doing just that. Like what the tobacco industry did for years, discounted studies that showed their products were addicting and harmful, for years they managed to hide their very own data on this and discount any science to the contrary.

The difference is that this effects many more major corporations. So the fight is going to be harder. The first thing Trump did in office was allow coal ash to once again be dumped in our rivers? What? Why? Because his friend owns a coal mine and you can save money by pumping it in a river over handling it in a safe more costly manor. It always comes down to this, just dump it somewhere and later, we'll get the government to clean it up for us and charge the public for it.

But, if you still want to ignore the many graphs about this, how about this, **we work towards cleaner air and water because that would be a worthy goal?** Apparently not to them? Could we at least do it for that reason? No, of course not! Because the news sources they listen to, corporate sponsored news, Murdock news, Fox does not want to go there. Their sponsors want to dump coal ash in our water ways, dump radioactive stuff in there too, because some very rich corporation will save a **little bit of money** that way.

If you don't want to stop it at least, why would you make it even worse by putting a tariff on solar panels?

Did you know that our vast military enterprises cause more pollution than many entire nations?

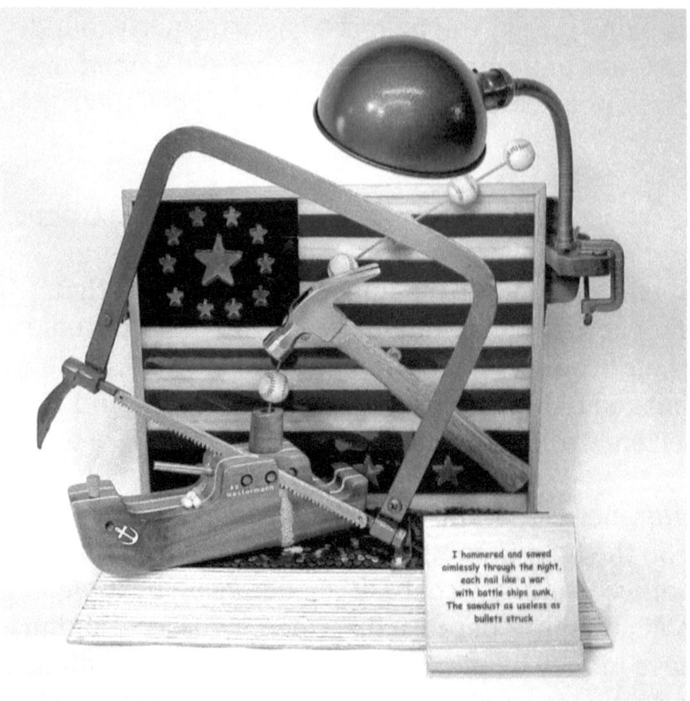

"The Never Ending War"

And you hear this, 500 climate scientists said that people causing global warming was a hoax (Just came around again today, but last time it was 30,000 of them). But when these things roll around ask to see who the "Climate Scientist" are, who signed it? Often it turns out to be people with no degrees. Or the same kind of scientists that said tobacco was safe. And you can also say this, I thought Republicans don't believe in scientists? When scientists say, there's no global warming, now you believe them? Really, you can't have it both ways.

But in conclusion, keep pushing the idea that it's a worthy goal to have clean air and water and the animals, who are often most effected, will love us for it.

Chapter 26

What did We do to Deserve 9-11

Many people don't really get into history and if you don't know history, you don't know cause and effect. Who done it to whom and who did it first?

So people ask, why did they attack us on 9-11? Well, did you know that we made a deal with the Saudis to get rid of Saddam Hussein? Did you know that we made deals with the Saudis to make sure Hussein's armies never returned to their country when we drove them out? And we would have bases there forever? Did you know that that war created the Jihadists?

I already mentioned, earlier administrations who put in the brutal dictator in El Salvador. The guy who was causing all the people immigrating from there to here. They should have a right to come here because our government had a hand in making their lives a virtual miserable living hell. And now, because of this interference in others countries, we get to enjoy long checkout lines at the airport for security. Republicans were afraid of lines at the doctor's office's? Well, many more of us have to stand in lines at the airport now and sometimes some of us gets examined just like you're at the doctor's office. Anyway, there are a lot of great books about all these subjects. People should read them. And a good place to start, Michael Moore's movie "Fahrenheit 9/11,"

In that movie Michael includes a list of many of the countries our government has messed with.

Here is his Partial list of Countries the USA has Screwed with.

1953 We over throw Minister Massadeq of Iran and Install the Shaw as a dictator

1954 We over throw democratically elected president Arbenz of Guatemala 200,00 civilians killed.

1969 We back assassination of South Vietnamese president Ngo Dinh Diem

1963 to 1975 America Military kills 4 million people in South East Asia

Sept 11 1973 We stage a coup I Chile. Democratically elected President Salvador Allende assassinated. Dictator Augusto

Pinochet is installed 5000 Chileans murdered.
1977 We backs military El Salvador 70,000 Salvadorians and 4 American nuns killed. CIA gives them 3 billion.)

1981 Reagan trains and funds contras 30,000 Nicaraguans die

1982 We provide billions in aid to Saddam Hussein for weapons to kill Iranians

1983 The White House secretly gives Iran weapons to kill Iraqis

1989 CIA Agent Manuel Niriega disobeys Washington then the US invades Panama removes Niriega 3000 civilian casualties

1990 Iraq invades Kuwait with weapons from USA

1991 We enter Iraq Bush reinstates dictator in Kuwait

1998 Clinton bombs weapon factory in Sudan, that turns out to be an aspirin factory

2001 to 2011 America plains to bomb Iraq weekly The UN estimates 500,000 Iraqi children die from bombs and sanctions

2000-2001We give Taliban ruled Afghanistan 245 Million in aide

2001 We give Osama Bin Laden expert CIA training on how to kill 3000 people in New York

2001Then President Bush invades Afghanistan to get Bin Lauden who is no longer there.

2001 Then President Bush invades Iraq a country that did not ever attack us.

2008 Then president Obama continues the war in both places even escalating for a time but it does not work. Afghanistan soldiers continue to kill the Americans who are training them. Those two wars become the longest running in US history. Killing or badly wounding thousands of American soldiers. And killing or maiming thousands of civilians in both countries. On coming home some 20 soldiers a day commit suicide.

Chapter 27

On Past Lives, Being Prejudiced and Karma

I need to mention this because it's important. The question of past lives is an interesting one. 60% of the population now believes that we have lived before and will be born again. In regression therapy, in psychology, they have also discovered people remembering that they lived before and remembering their past lives.

Now, there is no way to prove reincarnation 100%. The best you can do is have **indicators**. And there are lots of indicators out there, besides regression therapy remembering them, there are stories like this, a little boy insisting he was born in another city. The parents finally take him there and the boy points out the house he lived in and the people living there say they did have a son that died of a high fever, just like the kid said. The boy even knows where they hide their cash.

Then there is all those young people at age five or 6 who know how to play violin or the piano extremely well. And the people visiting another city they have not been to in this life, and feeling like they have been there before.

And then have a look at this, what are the proofs or indicators that you live only once? I have been searching and I have only found two.

One is the Bud commercial that says, "You only go around once in life so do it with a Bud." And the bible. But I have also heard from people that study the **original papers** from the bible, that it didn't say that either. And several people I've met, who study the Hebrew bible said, it's not in there either. It says, there is a reckoning, but the reckoning comes after many many lifetimes. But, if you have some other proof please let me know.

But the reason I bring this up is this, if more people new this, it would be better for all of us. Because if you new and accepted this, look how many problems would be solved. How could you be prejudice against woman, or other races, or crippled people if you knew you may come back as a woman or other race or a crippled person or you already have been one?

The best source for this, by the way, is in the Seth materiel, especially the first book, "Seth Speaks." What he points out in that book is this, there really isn't Karma, which some think means, you're sent back against your will to be punished for your negative beliefs and actions. But, Seth says, in the in-between life area, you yourself choose to be born as the race or sex that you had problems with so that you can learn what it's like to live on the other side of the tracks. You make the choice because the purpose of life is to **learn**. Sometimes you hear of a rich person pretending to be poor and living on the street for a few weeks, to see what it's like. But you can't really learn much that way because you know you're not there for long and soon will be back home in your comfee bed and swimming in the infinity pool once again. To really learn you have to really be in that life, that's why were made to forget before we come back.

So, I feel sorry for Trump. He will probably come back as a poor black slave woman working for a brutal master who rapes him has babies with him, but sells the kids off to be slaves to other plantation owners. And he is going to chose that life all by himself.

But, because these congress people think there is only one life, why should they care about climate change? They won't have to live through it, they think. So people are being starved in Yemen, they think they won't be born in Yemen or some other dirt poor country?

Also, because people don't believe in multiple lives, they think that if you abort a baby you are preventing a being from having a life. Now, if that was true, that would be a very bad thing. But that would also mean that every woman should have as many embryos fertilized as possible because just look at all those beings that will never have a life. And that cannot happen on a planet that is already over populated. Actually it's not over populated, it's just poorly managed.

But as Seth points out, if a being does not get born, due to an abortion, they will just pick up another body and be born anyway to someone else. You can kill a body but you can't kill the spiritual being that controls the body.

Chapter 28

The List of Crappy Things Trump has Done so far that Mostly Only Help Corporations

Once in a while, a Born-Again-Republican will actually ask me what Trump has done that's bad. It's amazing to me that they don't know! So, when they ask me this, I provide them with the list below and true to form, not one Born-Again I have sent it to every commented on it afterwards. I used to say this, "Name one thing the Republican party has done for the public in the last 20 years. And they never can give me an answer. Because they exclusively work for Corporate America now. They used to do things for the public. But now most of what they do is detrimental to the public's interests. Things like dumping sewage in our rivers and toxins in our air, keeping drug costs higher than any other country they sell those same drugs to. They get rid of regulations that later we find caused injury or death. Give tax breaks to the rich and take the money from programs for the poor.

Then when they make too bad of a mess, they have the government pay to clean up the mess. Things like the EPA changing one line on regulations of opioids that said, **only for temporary use, do not refill**. That alone was the cause of the opioids crisis. So we ended up with thousands of people getting addicted and overdosing because the prescription should never have been refilled! Now cities are going bankrupt trying to deal with the costs associated with this problem.

But I can't name one thing that the Republican party has done for us anymore, because Trump has actually done a few good things for the public that appear at the end of this list.

So here is the list of crappy things Trump has done so far that mostly only help corporations

The EPA posted numbers on hydrocarbons that scientists and researcher all over the country and world need. He stopped them from posting these numbers. **So if you don't see the hydrocarbons, they don't exist?**

He wants to cut meals on wheels.

He verbally attacked 4 minority members of congress telling them they should go back to their own country, when three of them were born here. *Calling others derogatory names.*

He attacks Elijah Cummings about Baltimore. *The guy who is investigating him.*

His continue siding with Putin over his own state department.

12 off his associates and son verified to have contact with Russians.

He has attacked the FBI and the intelligence community.

Instead of draining the swamp, he re-filling it with verifiable criminals who some of which are **now in jail**.

He lied about paying off porn stars.

His standing up with Saudis over a brutal murder of one of our reporters, now verified.

He not only denies climate change but makes it even worse by promoting coal and putting tariffs on solar panels.

He takes us out of the Paris climate change agreement.

He tries to defund renewable energy.

He allows coal ash to be dumped in our rivers again.

He lowered the rate of how much radioactive substances can be handled by lowering the standards.

He caused people in California to pay higher taxes than the rest of the country by capping deductions they have been able to take for paying state taxes.

He blamed California fires on poor forest management, when most of the fires were on land managed by the Federal government. He then wants to cut off FEMA money to California.

He wants to waste more money on the "Space Force" when we already have a bloated military budget

He stole money from his own charity.

He used donation money to pay for his own inauguration party.

He stood by Roy Moore. A verified sex offender and verified racist.

He has supported and not condemned Nazis and the Alt-right at the Charlottesville incident.

He puts people in charge of agencies who want to get rid of the agency he appoints them to, like Betsy DeVos and most of them.

His continuing to appoint unqualified people to government agencies.

His insulting foreign leaders undermining our stature in the world.

His Making fun of handicapped people on TV.

His harsh treatment of immigrants and their children people who have a legal right to ask for asylum.

His giving a ridiculous tax cut to the very rich that will cost us for years having to borrow money to make up for that tax loss and it will now have to take money away from programs for everyone else, like Social Security and Medicare.

He said during his campaign he would not touch Social Security or Medicare, then turns in a budget that cuts both.

When the middle class realizes his tax cut was mostly for the very rich, offers another for the middle class, but after the election, no mention of it.

He shuts down the government to get his wall by force, but does nothing about the many more people coming in with visas and staying. (*Just needs to implement E Verify to handle that at a much lower cost.*)

He ignores many other ways to stop drugs, like more x-ray machines that actually do stop drugs coming over the border.

He promises Mexico will pay for the wall, then hands us the bill and makes government employees suffer to get the money for it.

He promises a better and cheaper healthcare for all, then simply tries to destroy Obama Care instead, a program majority of people actually like.

He holds the all time record for lying, verified by numerous studies. Not to mention often verified in his very own tweets. (Trump Twitter Archive ;
http://www.trumptwitterarchive.com/)

He takes continuous golf trips and has events that coast us millions and enrich Mari Largo and many of the events are nothing more than political campaigns. <u>Violating the emoluments Claus.</u>

He complains about illegal's but hires illegal's immigrants at Mari largo.

He tries to interfere with a sovereign nations election, Venezuela.

He openly admitting to tax evasion.

He says the Muller report exonerates him but then won't let anyone read the full version of it?

He continues to openly obstruct justice by appointing Barr and not letting other people testify.

He takes us out of the Iran deal that was working. *Iran is now enriching uranium once again.*

He violated the emoluments clause by not divesting his business's, hotels that are now raking in money from the Saudis who are renting entire floors they don't need. *Is that a payoff?*

He wants to give top military secrets to the Saudis, the country who's people attacked us at 9-11

Makes no effort to get us out of Yemen where thousands of men, woman and children are being starved to death.

He lets, Puerto Rico, a US territory we are responsible for, still remain in shambles.

His having secret locked door meetings with Putin a country that verifiably tried to interfere in our elections.

He did nothing about trying to beef up security and voting machines so it doesn't happen again.

His asking Russia to illegally get Hillarie's emails for him.

His having daily contact with a news service and being too chummy with a news caster, Hannity. *A news service owned by a person from a foreign country.*

His continuous tweets apparently done to rile us up and cover up the latest investigation or charge against him.

Pulls us out of the nuclear proliferation agreement.

Rolls back Obama's clean water act

Hires John Bolton to National Security adviser a well know war monger would love for us to start a war with Iran.

I could go on and on with this list. And I assume he has done some good things too.

And there are some good things.

Fires John Bolton a known war monger.

He cut down the number of legal immigrants entering the country.

He has ushered in a golden age for women in the CIA

He tries to make peace with North Korea

He has secured the release of 19 people, including 16 Americans, from foreign captivity

He got NATO allies to kick in $12 billion more toward our collective security

Section 4

What Kind of a Government Have we become?

The long way home

Chapter 29

We are Headed for More Socialism

Every government **ism** will end if it has a flaw in the basic philosophy. That's not to hard to see for most people. Even in Daniel Webster Junior High School in the 60's they told me Socialism will award its citizens more benefits than it's working people can provide and then they'll go under. One new thing though that is changing that is the fact that we now have "automation." So more and more we ought to enjoy the fruits of robots replacing us and putting us out of work.

The fact is the more robots take over the less work there will be for people, so how are they going to be able to afford to buy things when you don't have a job? So one answer is this, if a company wants to sell products and services to us and also replace us or send our job out of the country, then they have to pay for the right to sell here. That's something we citizens own, **the right to be sold to**.

So we are heading for some kind of system where the government hands us some money so that we share in the bounty of robot labor. Uber, truck drivers, factory workers, trash trucks buses trains, fast food workers and even executive chefs can be replaced by robots soon if not already. Almost every other day we see a new robot taking over some job posted on Facebook. And their worried about Mexicans taking our jobs? They can even pick fruit and weeds. So we are heading for some kind of **Socialism** or there will be few left able to buy products or services.

Chapter 30

We're Seeing the End of Capitalism!

Boy, if you want to stir the hornets' nest, just post this on some site on Facebook about why some system like "healthcare" is broken. But how about Capitalism, can it end too?

Well, it's already happened, the very rich companies and very rich people, have taken over the government through campaign funding, so the politicians would do their bidding for them. The public, not being so organized, was not able to do much about it. Capitalism would ruin the only group that did have some power, unions. And before too long their very jobs were shipped out of the country too, without so much as a peep, because they weren't invited to the table.

And it didn't have to be this way. The flaw in our constitution was this, there should have been an amendment to the constitution that said, **Separation of Corporations and State**. And how is it that you can hand money to a candidate for his campaign fund? How is that good for anyone except the corporations handing out the doe? And to be able for a foreign government, like Saudi Arabia, to be able to hand them a million dollars for a one hour speech after they leave office? How is that good for anyone but them? Those things should have been illegal from the start. It was just recently that we found out congress could legally buy stocks in companies that they were making laws about.

So now here we are, the very rich getting huge tax breaks, the ability to dump their sewage in our rivers again. The news media controlled by a handful of people. Even radio has been ruined. Pacifica radio is the only radio station that is **fully** funded by the public. NPR and PBS now has commercials from corporations, so can they still tell the truth or ask the tuff questions? The stations all bought up by a few entities that play the same music over and over.

I called up KEARTH once to complain and amazingly they actually put on the phone the music director. I said, I'm so sick of Louie Louie and Sugar Shake, (Two songs they were overplaying at that time) Why do you keep playing that every hour it seems. She said, "Oh, we do surveys and those songs are very popular." Really, I said, how do you do your survey?" "Well we let people listen to 10 seconds of a song and if they like it, it's in. ?" I said, "That's not long enough, they're only going to pick the songs they are familiar with." So she says, "Well we also found out that people only listen for an hour anyway" I said, "Yeah that's why, you're playing tired and boring songs."

I happened to visit a friend that lives in Florida, and at that time anyway, there were stations there that hadn't been bought up by the chains yet and were playing music randomly, like they used to in the 60's, songs I had forgotten about and hadn't heard for years. In the evening I finally had to turn the radio off because the songs that they were playing were so good it was keeping me up.

Now a song like, Simon and Garfunkel's "Papa Hobo" would never be picked in that kind of survey. You have to listen to more of it if you've never heard it before. I have said the words to that song to many of my employees through the years (Because I liked to sing to them on the way to service calls) and none of them ever heard that song. I had to bring in my song book to show it to one employee, because he didn't believe there was such a song. It goes like this.

Detroit, Detroit
Got a hell of a hockey team
Got a left-handed way
Of making a man sign up on that
Automotive dream, oh yeah, oh yeah

And why is this? Because they only want people to listen to songs that maximize profits. Forget discovering new songs they've never heard before, screw that crap, they used to have disc jockeys that new the music and entertained us. And it doesn't matter what genre of music you like, country, rock or Jazz, they play the same songs over and over. I just never listen to music radio stations anymore.

And before the corporations took over, they would play different genres of music on the same station. You didn't have to go to a Country station for country or a Reggie station for Reggie, I mean you got introduced to different genres.

So that's what capitalism has given us, crap!

Chapter 31

So Capitalism Died Already,
Enter Crony Capitalism

I owned a small TV repair shop since 1983 and in the beginning it was a rocket ride, we didn't know what to do with all the money. Then NAFTA hit, trade agreements with other countries that allowed our manufacturing jobs to be exported, but also let in cheap crappy products. I realized then that slavery never ended in America, it was just exported to Mexico, China and even Viet Nam of all places. Countries where people worked at the point of a gun and had no bargaining rights, or holidays off, or vacations or sick pay.

But not only was manufacturing decimated in the USA, but also the service industry. Small businesses that repaired printers, air conditioner, cameras, TV's were going out of business all across the country. millions more jobs lost that also harmed the people who owned the shop they rented. There are empty small towns all across our country now.

I had two frat brothers that had opened a business that delivered fresh flowers to restaurants like the Chart House chain. They employing many of employees. It all ended when the economy sank because of all those manufacturing workers couldn't afford to eat out any more. Restaurants cut back and used dried flowers instead.

Another frat brother made the best car alarm with a failure rate of less than .2 percent. China's failure rate is, 10% and climbing. 35 employees lost their jobs when cheap alarms came in from China. Luckily for them, they had already made enough to pay for the building and some rental properties. So they did ok.

So that's what crony Capitalism has handed us. Without the protections I mentioned earlier, it's inevitable that Capitalism would try and take over the government for its own advantage. And Capitalism itself is stupid. I wrote the "Economic Formula" coming up soon in this book. Here is a brief idea what it's about. One major point in it is this, for a good thriving economy, corporations have to have their factories in the country they're in. You cannot throw your customers out of work and then turn around and think you can sell them things. I mean what are you thinking? And to only pay people .80 cents and hour in Mexico, because you're so freaking greedy? You're not creating a buying public there either! Why not just go out back, grab a gun and shoot yourself in the foot?

So here we find ourselves, Mitch McConnell welcoming help from the Russians so his boy can stay in office while they madly hand as much money and benefits as possible to their crony friends that put them there. **Capitalism is dead and it killed itself.**

Chapter 32

How Capitalism Destroys our Country and Harmed and Feeds off its Own Citizens

And now we end up with a government that is feeding off its own citizens for the purpose of turning a profit for its slave owners, Corporate America. Nothing changes here if it steps on the toes of profit for some company. Affordable healthcare, drugs, housing does not change because some corporation and their stock holders would lose money. 643,00 people go bankrupt each year because of healthcare costs. People have to drive across both boarders to buy the same drug in Canada or Mexico to be able to afford it. Every other country selling the same drugs for far less than Americans have to pay. Healthcare costing more and offering less than any other developed country. Even paying more than Single Payer would cost us.

DRUG PRICES: CANADA vs. US

Prices obtained Feb. 2018

	Canada	US
EpiPen for anaphylaxis	$250	$637
Crestor for high cholesterol	$224	$525
Premarin for estrogen therapy	$84	$494
Abilify for depression	$586	$2,718
Nexium for heartburn	$262	$506
Synthroid for hypothyroidism	$44	$114
Januvia for diabetes	$376	$1,307
Celebrex for arthritis	$254	$1,105
Advair Diskus for asthma & COPD	$361	$1,169

Thanks to Bernie for this chart

The interstructure falling apart and new and exciting future modes of transportation being suppressed, like clean sleek bullet trains. I met a young lady who got to my art show by Los Angeles's only subway line. She couldn't believe it only went 5 miles. In Europe they have over 6000 miles of subways. Clean new exciting industries not being embraced because the old technowledgy is making someone money and the blotted military budget. Which is blotted because it is making someone money.

The fast food industry harming its own citizens with food that lowers their life spans and makes them obese and why? Because those crops have been subsidized. They are largely the products of seven **crops** and farm **foods,** corn, soybeans, wheat, rice, sorghum, milk and meat highly subsidized that make **junk foods** cheap and plentiful.

Why don't they subsidize foods that are healthy for us? Can you imagine if organic foods were subsides and cheaper than regular foods? Look at the savings that would create in the healthcare industry? And why would you let people who continue to abuse their bodies with tobacco, alcohol and bad food be covered by healthcare? How about having an on staff health advisor?

Wallmart opened megastores all across the country that put small mom and pop shops out of business. Then when the town died, and everyone but the framers, local bar and gas station left, they closed the mega store. Anyone left would now have to drive 35 miles to the next Walmart. Big cities now full and dead small towns all across the USA. Watch the TV show American Pickers who often end up in these dead towns. Now Amazon is doing the same thing with out every having to build a mega store. Their finishing off the small stores in the big cities, like the one I owned for 35 years.

I was a Zenith Dealer since 1983 but laws got changed and now I found I could go to one of the big box stores and buy

the same TV cheaper than my dealer price from Zenith.
I called them and ask if I bought a 1000 of one model could I get
a better price and was told no. The big box stores are national
companies and they get a national price. I would have to open
stores in other states in order to compete with them. So only the
big guys were going to be allowed in the game.

But below is the formula that led to the condition we are
in. To change things you have to change the formula, it's not to
late but it can be done. In England and some other countries
they use a Boda voting system. You not only vote for the person
you like but also rank the rest of the contenders. So if say, Joe
has the most votes but does not get 51% of the votes, they take
the persons votes that got the lowest ranking and those go to the
second candidate that those people voted for. Now if Joe or no
one else still didn't get 51% they do it again with the second
person who had the least ranking votes distributed. So what you
end up with is the person who the most people ranked the
highest. If no one gets the 51% they do the election over again.

Arizona has implemented this idea, all campaign funding
gets pooled together. No candidate can spend more on their
campaign than any other. If they do, and they win the election,
the next person in line, that didn't cheat, wins the election. This
also means you don't have to be rich to run for an office.

But it's things like that would have to be done to change
things and there are people working on doing just that. That is
partly what this book is trying to accomplish.

So here is the basic formula that led to where the USA is
today. And it's pretty clear that to change things, you cannot let
the richest people or companies run the show by buying
politicians.

**The Basic Principles or Formula that Destroyed Capitalism
and our Country**

Corporations will end up owning and running the government for its own use.

They will use the government then to allow and form huge monopolies to keep prices high.

They will get the government to make trade agreements that will cause their employees to lose their jobs. (*Bush and Clinton, NAFTA*)

They will make it possible to ship jobs out of the country and not have to pay tariffs on those goods coming back in (*The main purpose of NAFTA*).

They will make sure, through congress, that wages stay low.

They will get government to deregulate so they can dump sewage in our air and water and allow poison in our food.

When it gets too bad, they will get government to pay to clean it up. (*Supper fund sights*)

They will buy up the radio and TV stations and control the media and work to not publish anything that exposes what they are doing (*Suppressing the fact that most shooting incidents are people on psych drugs. 6 companies now own most of the media*).

They will have politicians load the courts with judges (*Kavanaugh and many others*) that are pro-business and make laws that corporations cannot be sued or be fined for illegal acts. (*Currently they are trying to make class action law suits illegal and putting in their warranties that you cannot sue but must use arbitration, Chase did that on 8/7/2019*).

They will encourage laws that allow them to contribute as much as they want to political campaigns. (Citizens United, created by the Supreme Court, went out of its way to put that in effect. That wasn't even what that case was about, they chose to **write law** instead of adjudicate it.)

They will try to control the curriculum in public schools so we get good but dumb consumers.

They will be critical of government agencies like public schools, prisons, military and even the post office. Then they will try to privatize them so they can get their hands on all that money too. It will cost the government more and we will get less in return.

They will put out propaganda that Socialism is bad so people won't notice they are being screwed by Crony Capitalists.

They will attempt to control elections so there is little chance there guy won't get elected. They also contribute to the campaigns of both leading candidates to hedge their bets (*Currently cities are buying voting machines with no paper trail and Mitch is not letting bills be voted on that investigate voting fraud and to stop Russian interference hoping they will help keep Trump in*)

They will feed off their own citizens any way they can. They will start wars to help the military complex make money, over charge people for drugs and fight anything that could cut costs for its own citizens.

They will make sure laws against monopolies are not implemented of enforced. So they can destroy any new start ups because by buying in huge amounts they can out bid any new competition. (*Amazon was recently sued because if one of their independent sellers found a good product they would buy that product up and out bid them*).

Chapter 33

Is America a Liberal or Conservative Country?

This is a question that often comes up, where does the will of the people really lay? They always say we're a Democracy and I don't know why that is because we are not, we are a Republic.

The difference is this. In a Democracy if the majority of people on your street wanted to take your home and make it into a park, they could out vote you and just take it. But in a Republic majority doesn't rule. Representatives in the government, **ruled by the constitution,** protect the minority and poor so they can't be out ruled by a majority. So we are really a **Representative Democracy**.

But underlying that, the question is, are we more conservative or more liberal? And here are some stats that tell the story on various issues.

60% Want tuition free college.
70% Want Medicare for all.
59% Want free child care.
61% Want to legalize pot.
67% Want a fair minimum wage.
75% Think immigration is good for the country.
75% Don't own a gun.
58% Want to break up the big banks.
61% Want to lower the military budget.
58% Are concerned about the environment.
71% Are Pro Choice.
61% Are for equal pay for woman.
61% Are for labor unions.
(*Statistics compiled by Gallup, Pew, NRA, University of Maryland, Reuters and Progress for Change*).

So I'm not saying if it's good or bad either way, but we certainly are a leftist leaning country. So one has to ask, "why are both parties more right leaning then?" They don't seem to be working for the will of the majority of the people.

But it's not surprising either because most of the companies, who are really in control, are more conservative leaning. And he who owns the ball gets to make the rules.

And what happened to the Republican party? Here is the 1956 platform.
1. Provide federal assistance to Low-income communities
2. Protect Social Security
3. Provide asylum for refugees
4. Extend minimum wage
5. Improve unemployment benefit system so it covers more people
6. Strengthen labor laws so workers can easily join a union
7. Assure equal pay for equal work regardless of sex.

So their views have certainly changed, it's as if the party was liberal at one time. Now that they have fully embraced Corporate America, (as is happening with the Corporate Democrats as well), they care little about the needs and concerns of the citizens. So it looks like if you look at it through the eyes of Corporate American we are a Conservative country, but if you look at it through the eyes of the majority of citizens, we are a Liberal country.

Now if the corporations can figure out how to make a buck off of Liberalism then will all be OK.

Chapter 34

The Economic Formula

About The Economic Formula I wrote some years ago.

I'm including this in the book because this says a lot about our country. We have had all these great economists steer us this way and then that way and here we're still in trouble. If they actually new what they were doing, wouldn't we all be happy and in great shape? So, since that never ever happened, I had a look and broke it down to a simple formula. The great economists won't agree with this, like the Trickledown Theory by Uncle Milty Freeman, whose theory is really about transferring money from one group, the middle class and poor to the rich. A theory can usually be uttered just to steal resources. For years they talked about the trickledown theory, then when people got wise to that they modified it to, "we have to help the Job creators," remember that? Like as if, all the rich had businesses and were creating jobs so if we shower them with tax breaks, will have more jobs.

Mean while Uncle Mitt Romney spent his whole career buying companies, dismantling them and shipping them elsewhere. I mean what a con that was. So they couldn't say that any more. Now they don't say anything. Trumps tax break was billed as if it was for all of us, they just didn't mention it wasn't. That is till the last election in early 2019, when Trump screwed up and talked about a tax cut for the middle class. Spilling the beans on the earlier tax cut that was supposed to be for all of us, but no, it was only going to benefit the rich.

But ultimately since I wrote this, things are changing, as I mentioned earlier. Robots are taking over and there won't be enough jobs for everybody. So, my formula, although it currently is still workable, is eventually going to be outdated. Probably by some system where we share in the wealth that robots bring us, and that is really some kind of Socialist kind of government, now, isn't it? Now the formula.

The Economic Formula for a Consumer Based Society.

As a small businessman it has been a necessity that I study the problem of our dwindling economy and I finally came up with the following data regarding this. I've found the basic factors that make a growing thriving <u>consumer</u> based economy. There are only three. You need businesses that can produce goods and services that people need and want to buy and can afford. You need people with **disposable** income to buy those goods and services. And you need a currency that is stable. **These three factors alone make up an economic triangle.** And, if you raise one leg of the triangle the other two will rise. If you lower any corner of the triangle the others will fall. You can then see for yourself whether any of the "solutions" the great economists come up with will actually work or just make things worse.

Let's take a look at a stable currency first. We are talking here about the "value" of money, not the quantity of it. Money is really valuable only to the degree that it's backed by confidence. Since it's no longer backed by something inherently valuable, like gold. So, the confidence the world and public has in a particular government who prints the money is the main factor here.

If the government simply prints more money, that would not be an increase in that leg of the triangle but actually a decrease as the "value" of the money goes down, not up. So the only way to increase this corner is for a government to insure the money is backed by confidence, or lacking that, gold or some other valuable item.

You cannot have a good economy in times of runaway inflation for instance because business won't invest in countries that are in that situation as it's too risky.

Now, by **consumers,** we are stressing people with "disposable" income. Not just people with enough money to get by, but people that are well paid. So, the more "**disposable income**" they have the more they can buy. The more goods and services they can buy, the better the economy will be as long as those goods and services are **produced in that country.**

This of course could be overdone and people can be overpaid causing the price of a product to skyrocket or can even cause the business to go under and no longer be competitive as has happened.

Business's producing goods and services assumes that a company is making a product or service that people would need and want. It is also assumed they can make it in quantity without polluting the environment and killing off their consumers, or the cows. They would also need the people and resources to produce the product in abundance at a price that was viable.

So we see that for an economy to do well there must exist a balance between the companies and its employees. If the company does not pay enough to their employees, they will not have enough money to buy other companies products or services. The companies, over all, will then have less money, as we have been seeing happen now for many years.

And that leads us to the heart of our current situation. Our corporations, through NAFTA (North America Free Trade Agreement) and other trade agreements, have been making sure the US consumer makes less and less money by shipping jobs out of the country and paying those left less and less money.

This practice set in motion a **dwindling spiral**. Some say that it was not fair for a $30,000 per year insurance salesman to have to pay more for a car because an autoworker makes $70,000 a year (Never mind that the price of cars has not dropped since most of the manufacturing of cars left the USA). But, that $70,000 a year autoworker supported many businesses below him. Since he was a "**Consumer with disposable income**" he was able to buy cars, houses, lawnmowers, garden furniture, put his kids in private school, and could afford to buy insurance.

He also helped support the government by paying lots of taxes from income tax and sales tax. In other words, the money did trickled down under that scenario. All one has to do is look at Flint Michigan to see that this is true. The auto industry there kept the whole town going. It wasn't just the autoworkers who lost their jobs when General Motors sent their jobs from Flint to Mexico. And why doesn't Mexico now have a thriving economy since they have all these great jobs? Well, they didn't pay the workers the same high rate of pay or even a better rate of pay. $5.00 a day is not going to create a thriving economy or people who have disposable income.

How many cars do you think an autoworker in Mexico will be buying at .80 cents and hour? I'm not sure even Coke Cola benefited. Would you pay an hour's work for a can of Coke? Now the proponents of those trade agreements said that they were building markets in other countries. But the indicator of this is the **Trade deficit**, which continues to rise showing that they did not accomplish that either. The trade deficit shows that we are now a nation that imports, not exports. The only thing they successfully exported was lots of jobs and raw materials.

They also said that we were not going to be a
manufacturing country anymore. We would be a sales and
service country. Well, according to a recent article in the wall
street journal, in the last ten years over 50% of the companies
that serviced things like, TV's, cameras, lawnmowers, washers
and dryers etc, were forced out of business due to low prices of
the items they were repairing. Creating more consumers with
less disposable income. Not to mention a huge pile of waste.

Now on the surface this seems great. There have been
lower prices on "some" things, like TV's, VCR's, Camcorders,
microwaves, washers, dryer's etc. But along with that decrease
in price also came a decrease in quality and the longevity of the
product too. Most products are now made to last only two years.
So if you factor this in you will be repairing or replacing that
product sooner. So, it's questionable if the consumer has gained
anything in this area either.

According to this same Wall Street article, even if you
want to repair something it's getting harder to find someone left
to repair it. And don't forget the cost to the environment, with all
those now dumped TV's, VCRs and air conditioners filling up the
dumpsites with toxic waste. And we have seen recently that they
are being shipped and dumped to other countries where they
have now polluted their air and ground water.

The other problem is the cost has gotten so low in these
areas that sales are also affected. A few years before Wards went
under they were rated the highest seller of home electronics.
How does the highest seller go under? They couldn't make a
profit. My company use to make a $50.00 profit on a DVD for
example. Now the cheapest machine sells for $50.00. Now your
profit is only what, $10.00 at best? Now you have to sell 5
machines to make what you used to make on one. So the number
of units you sell may go up but your profit may actually be
decreasing.

And when people don't have good high paying jobs, there are not as many people able to buy as many of the higher priced units that they still make a good profit on.

Even the auto industry is crying that they no longer sell cars, they lease them. They would much rather sell them then lease them, as they have to carry the money for the loan. Then three years ago we saw the next rung on the dwindling spiral take effect, many higher paid office managers lost their high paying jobs as companies lost more money. Of course they lost money; they laid off "**consumers with disposable incomes**." Now these office managers will be buying less, causing the people and businesses they supported to do less trade, forcing another corner of the triangle to sag even lower.

Next on the ladder will be government jobs as the government pays its employees by income tax and sales taxes collected from working people in the private sector. We already see the government cutting back and making the fatal mistake of outsourcing some of these jobs to other countries.

Now it could have been true, what the proponents of these trade agreements were saying, if they had built markets in other countries and sold lots of goods and services it would have raised one leg of the economic triangle here. Or would it have? Since the factory was actually in another country and the product was made by people in that country the only benefit here would be those office workers and managers who they could not replace overseas or in Mexico.

Most of the money would go to the stockholders and the company executives. That would be an increase in income for some people. But these are people who are already well off and don't go out and spend all of their income. They just buy more stock with it or houses in the Hamptons. How would that have trickled down to the autoworker in Flint Michigan though? It won't. In fact, I think it was noted by someone that if all the wealthy people in the world distributed all of their money the rest of us would get a dollar each.

Now, how do you correct this? Well, businesses have to realize there is an economic triangle and therefore their income depends on the ability of their customers to have "**disposable income**." They have to realize that their own employees are indeed their customers as well. They have to stop being psychotic on this subject. They have to stop seeing employees as some nuisance that they need to get around somehow. When AT&T lays off 100,000 workers the executives at Ford probably think, "Their getting lean and trim, go buy some of their stock." When they should be thinking, "Holly Cow," their laying off our customers!

If their intention is to really build up a market in some other country, and not just abuse those countries citizens, with just more low wages and long hours, then you have to pay them enough to be a "**Consumer with Disposable Income**." As citizens we need to point this out to our elected officials, who in their mad scramble to get more campaign money from these same unthinking corporations who do everything possible to lose us more jobs. What we can do as shoppers is support local companies, buy American made products whenever possible and baring that, have things repaired by local service shops. Lacking this, the situation will continue to dwindle.

Appendix 1

Actual Things Trump has Said.

I just put this in for comedy relief. And in these times it's important to have some **comedy relief** in your life. Many TV shows fulfill that purpose, like **The Late show with Steve Cobar**, or the **Daily Show**. It is good to have a laugh when we are in a serious situation.

China Invented Global Warming

Laziness is a Trait in Blacks

Environmentally Friendly Light bulbs Can Cause Cancer

Mexico is Sending Over Rapists and Killers

Claiming He Could Have Prevented 9/11

It's freezing and snowing in New York--we need global warming!

We won with poorly educated. I love the poorly educated. "

Why can't we use nuclear weapons?

It's like a magnet. Just kiss. I don't even wait. And when you're a star, they let you do it. You can do anything. Grab them by the p**sy. You can do anything. "

Russia, if you're listening, I hope you're able to find the 30,000 emails that are missing. I think you will probably be rewarded mightily by our press. "

"I wrote this out, and it's very close to my heart. Because I was down there and I watched our police and our firemen down at 7/11, down at the World Trade Center right after it came down. And I saw the greatest people I've ever seen in action." — confusing 7/11 with 9/11, Buffalo, New York, April 18, 2016

Tells 3 congress woman to go back to their country when they were actually born here.

Can't we just nuke the hurricane?

Appendix 2

The Cult of Republicanism

This paper was my second attempt at trying to figure out why it became so difficult to have a discussion with Republicans. I finely figured out it wasn't everyone but just certain types of Republicans. And as you can see, I had figured it out, but had the wrong title. Although they do seem to be acting like a religious cult of some sort. I hadn't discovered the implant data yet though, that is all that is missing from this paper. And in the next appendix an earlier paper on how it has become so hard to have a conversation anymore. So you can see the paper trail here, my continuous attempt to figure this all out.

The Cult of Republican

I just had a major realization. I have been trying to figure out for years now why it has become so difficult to have a conversation with Republicans. And it just dawned on me, they're in a cult! The party has become a cult right before our eyes and right out in the public.

Their leaders are Hannity, Rush, Fox news, Prager and before that Glenn Beck (Who went so crazy even Fox had to dump him) not to mention all the A/M radio shows all across the country and internet news sources like Breitbart News.

So trying to talk to them is like trying to talk to a Moony or Born-Again Christian or Jehovah's Witness. It's like talking to a wall. And if you try to have a conversation and they realize, you're not one of them and saying the wrong thing or asking the wrong questions, You're immediately labeled a liberal or a democrat. Get it, if you're not with me you must be the devil.

And look how similar they operate. They make sure their flock does not read, tune in or listen to anyone who is in opposition to the Republican platform. And most of their members not only wouldn't think of listening to a Michal Moore movie, or read any of the numerous books critical of their party or its policies. And if you bring up one of these people's names you will be labeled a liberal or a democrat.

If you get in a conversation and make a valid point, again you will either be called a liberal or democrat or they will leave the conversation.

Cults often make their members disconnect from people who don't agree with their principles. 7 people, some close friends from college and grade school disconnected from me for simply trying to make a political point they didn't agree with.

And I also realized my list of, **How you know your living in a bubble (below)**, fit in with the cult idea just fine. The list should have been entitled; **You know your living in a cult if... So I just need to change living in a bubble to living in a cult.**

Man, I new this all along but didn't find the right label. I think this could make a fine book, **The Cult of Republicanism**. My ex pointed out that there are liberals like this too. So I have to research that.

I started by posting a comment on Facebook about whether we should get rid of the electoral college and posted this;
If it weren't for the electoral college we wouldn't have the best president ever Donald Trump!

And no one attacked me, they just thought I was making a joke, asking me if I was kidding.

Then I posted on another site with Trumps kids looking like Bevis and Butt head the following;

I think dragging Trump and his family with stuff like this is degrading when in fact they are doing such a fine job.
And same thing, just comments about you must be kidding, are you a comedian or something? Are you drinking?

So need to do more checking on that, but I did find this if you Google how to talk to a Liberal, you see a bunch of books and columns but there mostly by the same person, Ann Coulter. But if you search for, how to talk to a conservative there are all kinds of books and articles by many different people.

Anyway, if you have a chain on Facebook or emails from a liberal acting like I have described please let me know.

Appendix 3

The Death of Conversation

This is my first attempt to understand why it had become so difficult to have a conversation. I hadn't realized that it was mostly Born-Again-Republicans that you couldn't talk to.

The Death of Conversation

Definition; Conversation is a form of interactive, spontaneous

Communication; Between two or more people who are following the rules of

etiquette. It is polite give and take of subjects thought of by people talking with each other for company.

Conversation died today; its dead, burnt, deformed body ground into the sidewalk in a pool of blood that nobody noticed as they walked over it grinding their hard dirty shoes into its pitiful mangled face.

Today, I don't feel it's possible to intelligently discuss a subject with most people. What I perceive happens instead of conversation is that either they think they are already an expert on a subject and proceed to tell you why your opinion is wrong, or they offer a simple explanation and terminate the discussion right then and there.

I have suggested a piece of data to a friend who immediately went to his iPhone, not to look up the subject directly from the source and get more information about it, but instead went to a detractors site in order to squash it and tell me how wrong I was. On any subject you can find someone who will discount it. The detractors do serve a purpose and sometimes even are the ones with the correct information and they should be included in your research.

But that's not what's being done; instead the person ends the subject with the detractor's opinion without really finding out about the other side of the issue or even if the detractor is correct. Good honest research deserves more than that. In our court system both sides commonly use psychiatrists who sit there and refute each other. I was dismissed from jury duty once by pointing this out to the judge.

I had seen the death of conversation coming for a long time and only recently wondered what killed it? The art of conversation has been on its deathbed for many years. I thought back to my child- hood when I would sit spellbound listening to my parents, especially my dad having conversations about many topics. I can't really recall them ever having a heated argument although they must have had one on occasion.

And as I began to study the use of conversation today I realized that there were just a few factors that have led to its death. First was television. When I was a kid there were only 12 channels on our TV set and only 7 transmitters in all of Los Angeles. In the summer time you only had re-runs.

Looking back at our home movies I noticed that even though the TV might be on, people are still conversing. That never happens today, soon as the set is turned on the conversation, assuming there was one, stops. Could it be that TV just got more interesting?

Today we have over 160 broadcast channels and hundreds more cable and or satellite channels to choose from. And the mix is different, with how to demonstration shows, political and reality shows where there is an over-abundance of information. Not to mention that many people have the set on for many more hours of the day. We are inundated with data. So we are immersed in a flood of concepts to sift through and it's just very overwhelming.

Now consider the second culprit, the Internet. Now you have e-mails flying about and arriving in your in basket with even more stuff to sift through and much of it false. If you don't verify it for accuracy before sending it out you may be repeating false data to your friends. And inevitably one of them will check up on the information you sent and call you on it.

So it's dangerous to forward anything that has not been fully verified for accuracy. And if You're on Facebook you have even more information to deal with. That is why pictures with captions are prolific there. One Facebook group sends me about 5 pictures with captions a day, they spoon feed them out one point at a time. So it is no wonder people can't or don't want to have a normal conversation any more.

The computer has also created what I call the pseudo intellectual. This is a special type of person who may be highly educated or may have barely finished high school. They spend hours on the internet but unfortunately not always digging deeply into things. Like many people now they will go to some web site that is in opposition to the subject at hand and that is as deeply as they dig. Or more often they only go to sites that agree with their point of view and never go to opposing sites.

They don't have the time or inclination to fully understand a topic. There is no point to try to converse with them because they have already figured it out and for them to try to understand a new point on that subject means they have to re-open that can-of-worms again and re-evaluate it. And they don't want to do that because of all the other new data that is constantly coming in that needs evaluating.

One characteristic of this type of person is they use a blanket excuse that covers numerous topics. They might for instance say that all religions are bad or all metaphysics are practiced by quacks or one political party or the other is always wrong. This is a hidden standard that they have so they don't have to spend any time looking into these various subjects again. Or a common one is that only medical doctors can cure anyone and those that suggest using vitamins, homeopathic herbs or use acupuncture, are all bunk. Even though many of these subjects have been studied by scientists and deemed useful.

So this is great for this type of person because look at all that data that can now be skipped and not have to be thought about or studied. Just call it all bunk and you're done for the day. So you cannot have a conversation with this type on subjects that they have already pigeon holed, because all you will get back is their blanket excuse for handling that topic usually delivered with righteous indignation. You could possibly have a conversation with them on a topic you both know about and agree on however, as long as you don't stray too far off the beaten path. And imagine how frustrating this is when a person like this tries to explain away something to a person who has actual experience or expertise on a topic.

And the last thing I noticed is very few people have any training on how to carry on a conversation anymore. There are actually parts to this thing called conversing. What goes on as normal conversation between two people has become laughable at best.

Here is just one example of the many ways it gets trampled on. You bring up a topic but before you have finished the other person interrupts you with a long tirade on what he thinks You're talking about. But his point has nothing to do with what you started to say. The next thing you know instead of understanding your point, the conversation escalates into a heated argument. Having a conversation is different than having an argument.

Putting it simply, conversation means one person presents a subject, without interruption, then the other person acknowledges they heard it and then responds with data of his own and he too is not interrupted and his opinion is acknowledged. And so on and so on. Some people think that the purpose of conversation is to just get your point out and then squash the other person's point of view. That is really more like debating but even debating has some rules.

They also think that to understand a point means You're agreeing with it. Agreeing has nothing to do with it. All that is required is to "understand" the other person's point of view. That is what a conversation is and it does include etiquette. If they find that they have conflicting information, then go to the internet and get to the bottom of it if you can, sort it out.

So, what we have now is two people yelling over each other throwing out arguments that neither person is hearing and then the original topic being left and forgotten as the points drift off into new and unknown territory. Usually ending with both parties feeling upset, angry and miss-understood.

You can see this on many news talk shows now where one would think they would have guests who had the slightest modem of training in communication. And if You're brave enough to honestly analyze your own email conversations with people, particularly when discussing a topic that you're not in agreement with, you may see how these laws are being violated. If I make three points in an email I am lucky if I can get some people to respond to even one of them.

There are still people who know how to have a conversation but they are getting more difficult to find. But when you find one it is a real pleasure to converse with them.

And there still are places where one can learn the art of conversing, it is still being taught. Interestingly enough, if people had training in conversing most of the earlier problems I mentioned would be solved by that alone. (Hopefully not the end of conversing)

The End

Appendix 4

How to find out if you're living in a political cult

You're are living in a cult if you attack a person who has a different view then yours by saying they are a member of the opposite party, but you say it as if that is a bad thing and never realize that it's only your party that considers it being a bad thing.

You're living in a cult if you only listen to talking heads that you agree with and never listen to anything else.

You're living in a bubble if you're unable to admit that your party has ever done anything wrong.

You're living in a cult if you assume anyone being critical of your party must be a member of the opposite party and never realize that some people have an independent view and may not be aligned with any of the other parties either.

You're living in a cult if you think in absolute gross generalizations, I. E. Those liberals "Never" tell the truth or "Always" lies.

You're living in a cult if you condemn a president for doing something your president has done many times himself.

You're living in a cult if you can never admit that the opposing party has not ever done anything right that helped the country in any way.

You're living in a cult if you completely condemn any opposing celebrity, writer or movie producer but have never ever read or watched anything that person has ever produced for yourself.

You're living in a cult if someone makes a point against your party and instead of staying on point, you condemn that person for something completely unrelated that they may have done in the past.

You're living in a cult if you never check to see if an opposing idea is true or not.

You're living in a cult if you pass on data without ever checking to see if it's actually a fact.

You're living in a cult if you're presented data that condemns some aspect of your party and immediately blame the other party for something else instead of checking to see if the data is actually true or not.

You're living in a cult if you justify something your party did by pointing out the other party did the same thing.

You're living in a cult if you think everything that is wrong was caused by the other party and your party had nothing to do with it.

You're living in a cult if you don't like what someone posted so dismiss it by saying they must be listening to too much CNN, Fox or MSNBC.

You're living in a cult if your reaction to this data is to attack the person who wrote it.

Appendix 5

Recommended Sources of News

It is probably not possible to be completely unbiased, but one thing to look for in any book, or TV news show or movie is this. Can they be critical of both parties or both sides of an issue. If they can't you are most likely listening to propaganda.

Radio shows

Pacifica Radio
The only truly people funded radio in the country has many shows to offer and they can be all heard anytime on line. But here are some of the best and well informed shows. But, they are in serious financial trouble and you have to put up with way too many fund drives. Somebody please help them out!

Back ground briefing with Ion Masters
 On five times a week and he finds the most interesting people. Three per show. Well informed and interesting topics and people interviewed.

Thom Hartmann
He also finds the most interesting people and is an accomplished author himself. When he works on a book he reads everything including letters between our founding fathers. He digs in deep with his guests as well.

The Jimmy Dohr show
 On Friday at 5:00 PM. He slams both parties and

digs deep into issues in a humors way. Reminds me of Mort Sahl or George Carlin.

Ralph Nader Radio Hour
Ralph continues to be well informed. He also finds guests that are also well informed. Even though he has made millions on his books he gets up every day to work for America. For those who don't know who he is, he has been pointing out corporate deceit since the 50's. His first book was, "Not safe at any speed." Cars that would be totaled out at just a 5 miles an hour crash. We can thank him for safer cars, seat belts, padded dashboards and other safer products. So naturally he is shunned by most TV and radio shows. You cannot step on the toes of Corporate America and get on Corporate America owned TV, radio or newspapers. It would have been very interesting if his run for president succeeded.

Michael Moore's Movies
I can't say anything bad about any of his movies. "Siko" is full of data on our failed healthcare industry and "Where to invade Next," shows the shocking reality how far ahead other industrialized countries are with
Single payer healthcare, affordable education, government mandated vacation time and even school lunches. Fahrenheit 11/9 shows our sad current political landscape and sad daily lives compared to other nations that followed our lead and accomplished what we use to stand for.

<u>**TV shows**</u>

In these stressful times, with the kinds of Politian's we now have, it's important that you have some comedy relief in your life, that's the purpose of these shows. It's odd that the mock news shows more often tell more truth then the real news shows, albeit in a humorous way.

Real Time with Bill Myer

This is on HBO and he interviews 5 people per show. You can also check him out on YouTube. Although he is more liberal leaning he will go after either party. The last segment of his show, New rules," is very funny yet very insightful.

Fox news, Hannity and other hosts.

I watch various shows on this network but for me it's a comedy station. Don't think for a moment that anything you hear is accurate. I'm amazed at the audacity on how low they will go to spin a story. I think Hannity could convince his flock that zebras don't have stripes but spots instead, because if you look edgewise on any hair, it's actually round.

Sixty Minutes

Maybe one of the few TV network shows that is still allowed to let a little truth leak out on mainstream TV. They almost ate it when they were doing a story about how the tobacco industry was hiding the fact that their product was dangerous because one company had invested in NBC. Worth watching but they are not above bending certain stories either.

CNN

Only good for one side of certain news events like after a political debate. Anderson Cooper seems to be a decent fellow, but this is the kind of station that will avoid certain news and certainly some people like Ralph Nader or most of the authors of books I recommended. They are likely to only interview corporate democrats. I'm concerned with Chris Cuomo, he seems to becoming like Glen Beck with a Fox news kind of outlook but on the other side.

MSNBC
To me this is a pretend Liberal show, because they actually support the corporate democrats too.
So only good to find out how the other side spins the news. Not really a recommendation just a comment.

The late show with Stephan Colbert
Although a comedy show he often interviews some important guests. But also has a lot of fun with our politicians especially Trump. I get a lot of comedy relief from this show.

Last Week Tonight with John Oliver
Perhaps the funniest political talk show of them all. They have done so many funny things, like registering as a church and showing how much money flowed in. And they are perhaps the most researched show as well. A great way to learn something about politics and have a laugh at the same time.

Frontline
Has been doing investigative reporting for over 30 years on PBS. Well researched investigations.

<u>Books</u>

America, the Fare well Tour
By, Chris Hedges. He always has something

incredible to say about our current situation. Well informed and often interviewed on Pacifica Radio which means you won't be hearing him on CNN, or the nightly news or certainly not on FOX.

The Best Government Money can Buy.
 By Greg Palast, now turned into a movie, a fact filled book on how the corporations bought our politicians. How the World Bank and the IMF gut countries with economics alone and so much more. One of the last investigative reporters left out there and a great speaker.

The Dangerous Case of Donald Trump
Written by 27 psychologist warning us about the dangers of our president. They are really afraid that he has the attributes of someone who is mentally ill, a very dangerous person and could take us down with him.

Your Country Is Just Not That Into You: How the Media, Wall Street, and Both Political Parties Keep on Screwing You-Even After You've Moved On.
By, Jimmy Dohr. The title pretty much tells it all.

The Hidden History of Guns and the Second Amendment.
By, Thom Hartmann. Just one of his many well research books. He digs deep and reads everything about the subject including letters from our founding fathers.

Holidaze

A book of his humorous short stories about
vacations and Holidaze while growing up in
Culver City Ca. and being a single parent and
raising a child.

Assembled in America

A book about is career as an artist with
autobiography and 50 photos of his art work with
explanations.

The eBay Users Handbook
A step-by-step guide to posting items on eBay
with tips for increasing sales by a 18 year veteran.
Tips on maximizing sales.

The Rules of Running a Successful Business
After running a small business for over 35 years I
realized I new something about running a
business successfully. So I wrote it all down for
others to use.